THERE'S NO VACATION FROM DESIRE

THERE'S NO VACATION FROM DESIRE

BRUCE JARISH

Lyons & Grant
Multimedia LLC
New York

This book is a work of fiction. Names, characters, places, organizations, and incidents either are products of the author's imagination or are used fictitiously. Any resemblance to actual events, organizations, or persons living or dead is entirely coincidental.

Copyright © 2011 by Bruce Jarish

All rights reserved. Except as permitted under the U.S. Copyright Act of 1976, no part of this book may be reproduced in any form or by any electronic or mechanical means including information storage and retrieval systems, without permission in writing from the publisher. The only exception is by a reviewer, who may quote short excerpts in a review.

Published by Lyons & Grant Multimedia LLC, New York

visit our website at www.LGMmedia.net

Printed in the United States of America

Library of Congress Control Number: 2012933187

Paperback edition:
ISBN-13: 978-0-9837172-5-6

Contents

Chapter 1	....	*9*
Chapter 2	....	*21*
Chapter 3	....	*33*
Chapter 4	....	*47*
Chapter 5	....	*63*
Chapter 6	....	*69*
Chapter 7	....	*85*
Chapter 8	....	*97*
Chapter 9	....	*115*
Chapter 10	....	*127*
Chapter 11	....	*143*
Chapter 12	....	*149*
Chapter 13	....	*159*
Chapter 14	....	*171*
Chapter 15	....	*187*
Chapter 16	....	*201*
Chapter 17	....	*217*
Chapter 18	....	*227*
Chapter 19	....	*245*
Chapter 20	....	*249*

Chapter 1

I sat on my suitcase to close it. I told Lena anything remaining in the apartment she could keep. If she wanted to sell the furniture and keep the money that was all right too. We both accepted the inevitability of my going, especially since I'd spoken with my cousin James out in Monterey, California.

I just felt the need to run. I wanted testing. I wanted to do things with the things I already knew. I was getting away from love for reasons I didn't know or understand. Love had made me sick before, at Great Plains University in the Midwest, where I had my first encounter with it and that was only a few years ago.

But I didn't bother telling that to the fourth year Air Force Academy cadet sitting next to me on the commercial flight out of JFK. This was the first time I'd overcome my fear of flying. I've always rode in cars, buses and trains traveling back and forth from my Illinois college. I felt lucky to be riding with an experienced flyer. It was a security blanket for me. But once we took off, and the thrill of liftoff wore off, and everything was going along smoothly, the boy in the blue uniform fell asleep, and I was alone to figure out what the plane was doing and why it was doing it.

I began dreaming of a few years ago, because the pilot of our plane announced that we were flying over the Land of Lincoln where Great Plains University is, and where I played scholarship basketball, and where the coach would holler at anyone who was dogging it, "THERE'S NO VACATION FROM DESIRE!"

"What?" the cadet asked, waking, thinking I might be delirious or insane.

"I'm just thinking out loud about the country down there", I said, pointing out the window. "I played college basketball in that state."

"A little guy like you?" he asked, wanting to take the wind out of my sails, not wanting to hear me brag.

"You bet your life", I responded, almost expecting the question, knowing how to answer it. "I'd score ten to your two every time."

"I never played sports", he told me. "All I like to do is fly, get high and chase cunt. Nothing like flying and fucking in the wild blue yonder."

"I'm lucky I'm flying much less fucking up here."

"You're just not used to it", he said. "You'll be a lot easier on your next flight." I was impressed with the beauty and ruggedness of the mountains. I was going into virgin territory. I'd never been west of the Rockies. West of the continental divide no one ever got their hands on me. Hardly anyone knew my name. I could be as unknown as I wanted to be. Once the jet didn't leave its shadow on the farmers dell anymore I knew there was something else. But I was carrying around too much love baggage. I couldn't stop thinking about Lena, even though I knew when I stepped off the plane I'd have plenty to think about. I'd have to do everything for myself, and in a hurry, before my money ran out.

James was supposed to meet me at the San Francisco airport. I saw the blue endless Pacific. We circled the Bay City for a few minutes, and from the low altitude it appeared to be the city of white, and the city of hills that I imagined it would be, from all the photographs I'd ever seen of the place. I was not disappointed with the aerial view.

I felt the first part of my expedition got off to a perfect start. I also had the feeling that no matter what happened, no matter where I was, no matter how far the distance, it only took a few hours to get here, and

THERES NO VACATION FROM DESIRE

in that amount of time no change could be produced that could make my world different.

Although I had the feeling I was thousands of miles away from home, it still seemed, in terms of time, a very short distance. If I'd used a car this morning and had decided that the new land was north, I might be in the Catskill Mountains now. So the jet couldn't change the illusion that I was still very close to the east coast, only hours, and the east coast was what brought me to this running scared position, and I wanted to feel safe.

James was waiting for me at the terminal when I arrived. Although the last time I saw him we were both four years old, and I couldn't remember the meeting, he said he'd be wearing a cowboy shirt with fringe pockets, along with a small brimmed sombrero. A full face mirror sunvisor would be clipped to the front of the sombrero.

James' father was my father's half brother who had settled in California after returning from combat in the Pacific after World War II. Although my uncle was well liked by his New York brethren he was always criticized for rarely returning to the East for weddings, funerals or any other family events. I didn't even know he was dead when I called James out in Monterey after getting his phone number from information.

It was a long shot calling James, but he was the only person I knew alive in that time zone, and the chance paid off. I had heard a lot about James as I was growing up, and right through college, because he had some trouble with the law. As a youngster he was a runaway. He'd even spent some time in an institution for a nervous disorder. From what I saw of him now he seemed to be making up his mind to be either a psychedelic Mexican or hybrid of all American cultures that has mixed California into the population it now is.

James was a talented athlete. He played football at San Diego State. Seeing him there now I didn't know how he managed that because he didn't have big college size. Even though small for a lineman, he was still heavily recruited. He ended up at San Diego. Back east we were proud of his athletic career as we got word of it.

I wore dark slacks and a white shirt and blue tie like I told him I'd be wearing. We recognized each other, although I hadn't seen his face because it was covered with the mirror, and it didn't appear like he was going to remove it. When I stared into his face as he spoke I only saw my own reflection. "Made the ride up especially for you", he said warmly, giving me the interlocking thumbs hippie handshake. "Do you remember the time we killed that cat in the alley in back of your house?". "No", I said, not wanting to disappoint him, but realizing that I might have a big problem here. I didn't remember the cat and I never had an alley in back of my house.

It was a well designed little airport. James took the time to tell me that his father had died within the last year, and that he didn't have any relatives living in the state anymore, only back in New York City. "But I'm set up good in Monterey. I've been teaching math there for two years. They wanted me to coach football, but if I can't play I don't want to have anything to do with the game." I kept wishing he'd lift his visor so I could see what he looked like. It seemed he got so accustomed to wearing a face mask when playing football that he felt incomplete if he wasn't wearing one now.

Driving south, leaving the San Francisco city limits in James' mid-sized pickup truck, I said, "You said there were some jobs down there?"

"Yeah. The faculty meetings start soon. I've already been in touch with the principal."

"You told him about me?"

"Yeah. He wants to talk with you. He said he could use a person in his special education division." Although I wanted to stay in the gym and was disappointed with what James told me, I was still glad to know that an income may be mine soon, and that was more important than anything else at this stage of the game.

"I have to pick up the drugs in San Jose. It's on the way. You don't have any place else to go to now, do you?", he laughed, scratching his face under his mirrored visor. "I need the stuff to calm me down. The only things better than drugs are equations and drums." I thought he was talking about the aftermath of his nervous breakdown, the calming effects of the drugs, and expected him to stop at a rehabilitation clinic. But he stopped in front of a cottage on the outskirts of town and asked me, "Anything in particular you want?"

"No. I'm feeling fine." I knew I'd better inure myself to this guy very quickly.

His late model pickup truck was black. His salary was good. I sat at the curb in the truck near a palm tree while my masked cousin walked out of the cottage that was surrounded by a low brown mountain range in the not too far distance.

He put the package on the black front seat vinyl, between us, and said, "A little weed. A little coke. And just to make sure, a little acid. Hell, you're the first family I've seen since my old man kicked off. Welcome to your new home."

"Thanks," I said, repelled by his underworld greeting.

James finally removed his sombrero, and he was movie star handsome, even though he wore an unconventional crew cut, and his face, under his eyes, was thickly lined with shoe shiny black stuff, the way football players wear it in the afternoon sun to reflect the rays away, to prevent squinting.

"Big game coming up?" I asked him, joking, talking about the thing that terrified me most about him.

"Yeah, the biggest," he said, not looking at the road now.

"You think you can take my best shot?" he challenged.

"I doubt it," I said, "we played different sports." I made up my mind never to provoke him into showing me how hard he could hit.

Continuing south along the eighty mile drive, the coast was beautiful. The scenery gorgeous. We rode along, mostly talked out. James was asking me questions about relatives he knew of in New York but had never met.

"I have to make a phone call later," I said, "Can I do it from your place?"

"If you get time and charges and pay me on the spot," he said, as though he'd been beat for money in the past.

"I was about to suggest the same thing," I told him.

"That's alright. We think the same way," he grinned.

In Monterey James lived in a huge three family house with a small lawn in front. There was one apartment downstairs. Two up, after climbing a rear sturdy wooden staircase. The big backyard, which faced the interior of the town was defined by a white picket fence, and there was an active rabbit pen next to it. I'd never seen a lemon tree before.

His neighbors' entrance was only a few feet away from James' door. There was a Marine Corps emblem glued to the upper part of the door window. "Ralph lives there," James told me. "He just retired from the military a couple of years ago. Got a nice little Japanese girl living with him. I think she does housework around town. Ralph don't talk that much for a friendly guy."

The small carpeted living room we entered was dominated by a wall poster that hung in the corner. It was an aerial view of the southern, pointed tip of the Monterey Peninsula. James indicated an area on the chart and said, "That's Lovers Point. That's where I go to the beach."

In addition to the poster there were candles sporadically placed about the room on tables, and a case of football trophies that might've brought him a pile of money if he'd hocked them. But the most outstanding feature of the place was a set of drums in the middle of the room. They took up so much space that to move about you had to walk around them with your back to the wall. It was a permanent fixture James told me when I asked him about them. He played double bass, multicymbals, tomtoms and a snare. "I beat the hell out of those suckers," he half grinned, grabbing a drumstick then putting it down.

I called Lena in New York. She was very happy to hear from me, although I could tell from the tone of her voice she was depressed and not feeling well.

"Yeah. He met me at the airport."

"Does he have the job for you?"

"I think so. I'll find out in a few days. How are you though? How do you feel?"

"Terrible," she whined. "I miss you more than I thought I would. I wish you were here. When are you coming home?"

"But I just got here," I said, feeling a bit peeved. "Let me do something first for Christ sake!" Taking the irrational bite out of my tone I continued, "I don't know how long I can take it without you." I didn't want to get overly sentimental with her though and altered my tone once again and told her in a matter of fact way, knowing it would soothe her, "I'll know about the job soon. For now I'm staying here with James. There's nothing to worry about. By the time you get here I'll have my own place so we can be by ourselves."

She started crying as I started hedging that the call was costing me plenty and that maybe we should talk another day. "I'll write you a letter tomorrow and tell you when I'll call again," I said. Then I gave her the number I was calling from.

"Goodbye love," she said.

During the time of my conversation with Lena, James was sitting at a table with a handful of shiny wooden drumsticks tapping out a rhythm on a little rubber pad, instead of hitting the drums.

"What are you doing?" I asked him after hanging up.

"Writing a song."

"I didn't know you had writing talent?" I said as he continued tapping.

"I can write something new every day," he said. "The well never runs dry. Maybe I can get a little band together some day. I like beating my drums more than anything," he declared, putting the pad away, sitting on a small stool that was part of the drum arrangement, thumping out a simple beat on the tomtom. When he finished he said, "You want to see the town?"

"Sure," I said, a little more confident in his behavior since I realized he was more eccentric than dangerous. He was a many faceted misfit. "Yeah," I said, "Let's go see the town."

If I hadn't seen and lived in small college prairie towns in the Midwest, and had no idea of what places like that were like I would've been disappointed. But knowing what to expect the countrified village didn't bother me. This was the type of atmosphere I was looking for. I came out here to live. To find a place to settle down and enjoy myself.

Some of my best and worst times happened in those rural plains towns. Irregardless of whether those experiences were positive or negative, they made me live. They forced me to go the gamut of feelings almost every day. My first love was in a small town. When she ruined my spirit for a time by being unfaithful that was the liveliest deadening experience I've ever had.

So cruising along Alvarado Street in old Monterey it felt just like a small Midwestern town to me, except we were on the warm weather Pacific Ocean coast. The moonlight magnified the beautiful Santa Lucia mountain range encircling the town. One of the best things about Monterey is that it's surrounded on one side by the ocean and inland by the mountains, cutting off all possibility of urban sprawl. The only way they can improve the town is by making changes where something else already exists.

My guide was proud of the town and pointed out things to me as we drove along on the coolish night with the windows half opened, playing the radio. The biggest building on Alvarado Street was the old fashioned high rise San Carlos Hotel. Immediately beyond the hotel was the ocean and tourist district, the wharves.

James drove us out onto the L shaped municipal wharf where we could get away from shore and look in at the town, and at the tourist center Fisherman's Wharf, which was still bright and lively with busy restaurants, tourist shops and fast food stands. Fishermen were readying their nets in the marina for a night catch.

"Tomorrow night I'm buying you dinner at the Swordfish," said James, nodding towards Fisherman's Wharf. "Did you ever eat an abalone steak?"

"What's that?", I asked him, thinking it was something like baloney.

"Shell fish. The sea otters love them", he said when he heard the slick playful creatures grunting out on the rocks in the bay.

Although James had purchased all those drugs up in San Jose he still didn't do anything with them. They were still in the glove box of the truck.

"You want to smoke now?" he asked, starting to roll one.

"Time's right," I answered. But just then a blazing flash from Fisherman's Wharf instantly lit up the entire town, and my first clear illuminated look at the village was through a devils light.

"It looks like a fire!" James shouted, ditching the weed, starting the truck, and driving in off the municipal wharf and coasting as close as he could to the tourist wharf, where he said, "The Palace is burning!"

It was the oldest and most famous of the restaurants there, a land-

THERES NO VACATION FROM DESIRE

mark. We sat there and watched her burn as the firemen tried their best to save her. But when we saw the pictures in the morning newspaper the only things remaining of her was her burnt out hull and charred spiles sticking up out of the water.

Chapter 2

Monterey Bay is shaped like a half moon. The bottom point is where the town of Monterey is located. The top point, about forty miles away, is Santa Cruz, where the state university is, and where I had to go to get a teaching license. It's a straight drive north along the Pacific Coast Highway. On a clear day you can see the Santa Cruz Mountains from our second story veranda in front of our house. We lived a few blocks from the bay.

After adjusting his headgear-visor James said, "It's one of the best towns' on the coast. There's a big park there. Like Coney Island back east. Here, listen," he ordered me, slipping a cassette into his tape player, and The Doobie Brothers sang Neal's Fandago. Approaching the visual scene in the song it seemed to be like Monterey in terms of size, but where as Monterey is a working mans town, Santa Cruz is collegiate, dominated by that not pushed around by the world atmosphere.

"You should've seen this place a couple of years ago," James said. "It was the hippie capital of the coast. Better than the Haight. In sixty-six they voted in a hippie mayor. Freaks walked around the streets getting stoned and not having to worry about it. No busts. I wish it was like that now."

"Why? You seem to do what you want to anyway."

"That reminds me," he said, snapping his fingers. "Maybe we should take a ride over to San Jose when we finish here?" I was beginning to get comfortable with him and asked him things that I wouldn't have just a few days ago.

Before we left the house in the morning James pounded out a ten minute drum solo causing his immediate neighbor next door to blast the Marine Corps Hymn out on his stereo.

"We like it that way," James told me when I asked him if he was bothering the retired marine.

"We wake each other up. Get used to it. We do it all the time."

"What about the people downstairs?" I asked, "don't they complain?"

"What are they gonna say?" he answered, putting on a white foamy forearm pad, taking a few swings at the paint chipped kitchen door, working up a good sweat.

The town of Santa Cruz took great civic pride in itself, and was immaculate in spite of its reputation as a stronghold for overage hippies and the new ones attending the university there. The showcase of the towns self love was a five block long mall through the heart of downtown. Palm trees, benches and year round water fountains, combined with the salty scent of the ocean and the green surrounding forests made Santa Cruz feel like a paradise. The central coast was all an Eden to me at this time, even though James told me that the rainy season would be starting soon, during the winter months.

Although I was to meet Mr. Sender, the principal of the school where James worked in Salinas, the opening of school was not quite a couple of weeks away and I had plenty of time to get things squared away, and getting a California teaching license was the first order of business.

"How do you like the University?" my seemingly knowledgeable guide asked me.

"Where is it?" I said, scanning the area we were driving through, feeling as though I was still in the forests of Big Sur, which was where

THERES NO VACATION FROM DESIRE

James took me yesterday.

"Look through the trees," he said, "and you can see the buildings."

"There's too many trees to see through here. Where are we?"

"We've been on the campus for five minutes already."

The sprawling campus was so well built into the countryside that if you didn't know it was there you'd never be able to find it by passing through. He steered the truck up a narrow dirt trail that seemed to be taking us to some backwater lagoon. Within moments though a three story blonde brick building came into view, and James said, "The licensing division is in there."

I liked the surrounding area so much that I didn't want to do anything official, and said, "Why don't we just look around and get this done some other time?"

"You a damn tree hugger or what?" was his harsh unexpected reply. "You think I'm your private chauffeur?" James continued.

"No, but."

"No buts!" he snarled madly. "You can't even TALK to my man if you don't have your credentials."

Embarking from the maniac's auto we walked along a winding path sole deep with cork like wood chips that led to the entrance of the building. It was a beautiful structure that didn't seem like it belonged here though, like it was dropped in from a helicopter.

As soon as we entered the air conditioned lobby James removed his headgear. I was surprised to see he wasn't wearing the black wax under his eyes, like he did when he knew he'd be doing a lot of driving. Classes hadn't started yet and there were only a few people walking around, most of whom looked like maintenance men getting the place in shape for the next round of students.

We found an information room with a sign on the door that read "OUT TO LUNCH." "What do we do now?" I asked James.

"Keep looking, They're always out to lunch."

We didn't have to search for long because an attractive girl wearing a rainbow headband around her long blonde hair entered the lobby. We stood dwarfed among the realistic murals depicting the giant redwoods. We approached the girl with questioning faces, but instead of saying anything, she stood there bashfully and smiled, as though silence was the proper way of greeting people here.

"We're looking for the teacher licensing division," I said to her.

"We think it's here?"

"No. You've come to the wrong place, here," she said, leading us to a huge wall map of the campus. It appeared to be all terrain and no buildings. But when she started pointing out the black dots that represented the learning areas I could see that instead of being in some isolated little wilderness camp we were right in the middle of one of largest and most prestigious academic centers in the state, just like James said it was, but which I couldn't accept until I'd seen the evidence.

As she was giving us the valuable information James was rudely questioning her, because he didn't trust her, and thought she was leading us on a wild goose chase.

"This is the exact place I got my license", he snapped at her, so incensed by nothing that he offended me too.

"No. It was never here," she corrected him politely, though taking a step back, James' posture being very aggressive. After he was proven wrong he put his headgear on and wandered about the lofty lobby checking out the sun's rays pouring in through a stained glass window design of the Golden Gate Bridge.

"Hey James', I called him, as the pleasant girl was about to point out on the map where we had to go.

"What?" he hollered from way across the other side of the cavern of higher learning.

"Come here, will ya, and take a look at the map. We have to go someplace else." The girl showed him on the map how we could get to the building we wanted, since it was on the other side of the campus.

"Oh yeah," James said, calmer now. "Yeah, that's the place I thought was this," he said, getting himself out of his mistake as gracefully as he could.

We climbed aboard his truck and headed out. I still felt more like we were going camping than license gathering. I had something on my mind and wanted to spill it though.

"Now I remember," he said, though his tone unsure, turning down the radio so we could talk each other into the right direction. I said angrily though, not being able to hold it in anymore, "What's the matter with you? Don't you know how to talk with people? She was only trying to help us." I could sense him grimace and make a face under his visor, and I hoped he wouldn't turn violent on me.

"No women in the locker room," he spit out rotely.

"What are you talking about? You're fucked up. I'm surprised she didn't call security on us. You looked like you were going to slug her. Get locked up for nothing."

"Better luck next time!" he roared, fogging the lower part of his visor.

After five minutes of riding James turned onto a gravel road that led to what looked like a campfire pit, and said, "The place must've burnt down."

"I think your place must've burnt down," I said, still angry from our discussion and still not getting to where we wanted to. I was beginning t o lose confidence in my cousin in spite of the things he could do and had done.

"There was never a building there," I continued, "There's not even enough there to be the remains of a dog house."

"Well, from her directions and map," James said, seemingly under control, our dispute forgotten, "this is the only place it could be. She was lying to us, Jack. The licensing division was in that building. She put her wing in motion taking us away from the true flow of the play."

"What are you, nuts or something? Why would she send us out in the woods when it's her job to help us find the place?".

"I play by instinct. She was lying."

"Then use your damn instinct and find the place."

We backed out of the driveway onto what looked like a main road again, but when we scanned the hand map we couldn't figure out where we were.

"This is like being in college again," I said, "Always the wrong information. You can't figure anything out."

THERES NO VACATION FROM DESIRE

James stopped near a shaded tree stump big enough for both of us to sit on. We smoked a doobie and looked at the map together. It was so lonesome and empty there we felt like we were on a Pacific island and our only goal was to keep our spirits up till we could be rescued. We checked out all the options and still couldn't find an out.

Stoned, for awhile we forgot about the business of the day. James went to his truck, and from under his seat took out a rifle, and aimed it at the top of a tree, getting his eye in focus. "What's that for?" I asked James, "This isn't a real wilderness, only an academic wilderness. You learn more on your way to class than you do in class."

"I thought I heard something in the bushes," he said, "Maybe a bear."

"Here? Nah! Go on ! Let's find that building before we get into trouble."

"I'm preventing trouble. Nobody gonna fuck with us. First that girl sent us packing in the wrong direction and now we're lost in the woods. If anyone's stalking us they're going down first."

"Hey, don't act crazy," I said, "Take your mask off and show people your face."

He pointed the rifle at me, point blank, and cocked it. "You don't know me!" James hollered. The cocked gun was pointed between my eyes and I was so scared I wanted to scream, but I didn't want to set him off.

"We just made a mistake," I said. "If you killed me it would be like killing yourself."

"Don't give me any lectures," he rasped out in a severe monotone. "You've been knocking me ever since we left the girl", James continued with great concentration. "What do you know about the country out here and how the people are."

I wanted to rebel and do him some harm for threatening me, but he was sick and he was in charge and my only way of getting out of this alive was by complying with his every wish at this time.

"Don't you give any orders around here. Understand? Is that clear?"

"Yeah," I said, thinking I'd find a new place to live as soon as we got back to Monterey. I even thought about taking the bus back.

Then James said as though nothing at all had happened, "There's no bullets in the damn thing. I just wanted to see what you'd do. I had to be sure. You didn't flinch at all. Good man."

But James flinched when a two man armed security force entered from the woods with their pistols out of their holsters, yelling, "Freeze! They'll be no shooting here. We're taking you in for possession of an illegally loaded weapon."

"Hold on there, mister," James said, dropping his rifle to the ground. "My gun has no bullets. Check it out. I didn't do anything wrong. My New York cousin's a photographer. I was trying out some poses to send to my relatives back east. His camera is in the truck. See it hanging on the rifle rack," he pointed.

"We're only looking for the Sloan Building," James continued. "We got lost out here and were waiting to see if someone would come along. We were just killing time."

Although the security men were wary they realized we reacted in a peaceful sane way, and were more than helpful telling us where to go and how to get there. Within one hundred yards of the campfire site was our destination, which is where the security men came from when they saw James' truck stopped in the woods.

Once we found the right place to go to our problems were over. The licensing division was in a recently constructed building, one that James had never seen before. The office procedures were professional and quick.

THERES NO VACATION FROM DESIRE 29

Since I already held a teaching license from the state of New York, and California and New York use a system of reciprocity in these matters, my new license was awarded me in lieu of having my junior college and college transcripts sent to them.

I filled out the forms requesting the transcripts right there, and they even paid the postage. I was told the license would be mailed to me as soon as possible, and it wouldn't take very long either. "Probably only a week or two depending on how fast your records get here."

The next step in developing myself into a state of freedom and independence was meeting Mr. Sender, the principal of the high school James worked at. When James called his office he found out from the secretary there that the chief was attending an academic conference in Los Angeles and wouldn't return until a few days before school started, leaving me two weeks to do nothing.

After getting this information I became unreasonably angry with James, saying. "You told me for sure I'd get to see the guy and now he's giving you the brush off". I didn't raise my voice though, not wanting him to run for the rifle again, because the next time it might be loaded. James was getting as used to me as I was to him, and he answered me easily, saying, "I'll get you in the door. Don't worry about it. I didn't say when, but I'll get you in".

The next few times I spoke with Lena on the telephone I had to tell her that nothing was for sure yet, and for her to hold on. "Maybe, why don't you come out here around Christmas so we can work on a tan. That would be a holiday you'd never forget," I told her. She didn't seem very enthusiastic though unless I had some security for her. Our letters to each other were rich with words of love, but since James was usually around, getting time and charges whenever I called New York, we didn't get a chance to say important things to each other.

The sun was really beginning to bother me after a few weeks, after not seeing one single cloud in all that time. These were days when nothing seemed to be working out. Although friendly with each other, James and I went for a day or two every few days without speaking with each other. When he played his drums I usually sat out in the back yard. He'd be at it for hours. It was a great physical release for him he told me. When James wasn't banging the drums I noticed he was always working with equations. There were scraps of paper all over the apartment with numbers and equal signs and signs I didn't understand on them.

"Boning up for school?" I asked him, thinking he was refreshing his mind with all the old formulas for a new group of students that would be his.

"No", he said. "I use equations to write music. I never taught myself to read music. It was easier to do it this way since I already knew how to use the math."

"But no one else can read it. Right?"

"After they hear it they can put it down in their own terms. Want to know how it works?"

"No", I said. "I like music too much to change it into math", remembering the trouble I had with the subject, but thinking that this was the first time I'd seen the arduous discipline used to reach such pleasurable ends.

"Math is weight lifting for the brain," James said, defending his subject. "It can be applied for any use," he concluded.

An assortment of drugs was always around and being used. While listening to James play his drums I dreamed of New York and what the days are like there. Since California sunshine is constantly telling its citizens to "Have A Nice Day" I thought about the buses on Madison Avenue with the lights flashing in front telling the citizens of the city to "Have A Nice Day" too.

Things weren't working out as fast as I thought they would. I was becoming depressed, becoming miserable, and felt like running home to Lena, something she encouraged whenever we spoke. I missed her so much I retrogressed into tripping on acid with James. We sat on a bench in the Spanish Plaza near Fisherman's Wharf for eight hours. It was a bad trip for me though, because the damn sunshine kept talking to me, telling me to "Have A Nice Day". I got to the point where I hated sunny days because they were a cheap commodity. There were bad days I needed bad weather to coincide with my nature. It would've been a relief to have had that. Because when I wasn't feeling alright the "Have A Nice Day" sunshine made me feel like I was the only one out of whack.

Events started rolling again in early September. When James returned from a faculty meeting one day, he told me I had an appointment with Mr. Sender, and that now, because I already had my credentials, I could start working immediately.

"See," my cousin said. "You took care of the other stuff first and now he'll hire you on the spot. I promise." The only tangible evidence I had that I was getting anywhere was the receipt of my license from Sacramento, the state capital. It arrived in a big brown envelope. All the information on the credential was correct. It had only been within the last few years that special education had become a separate field of study. My license for physical education qualified me to work as a special educator.

It was a big certificate. If it didn't stain it could've been used as a place mat at the kitchen table. Under the typed in information that pertained to my particular set of circumstances, the official seal of the state was embossed. The seal was round, and bordering its outer edges read, "The Great Seal Of The State Of California". At the center of it is an image, and over the image it says "Eureka". In the foreground of the scene is a lone Indian. He's sitting, wearing a war helmet with a plume in it, and he's holding a spear in his right hand. A dog is sitting and resting at his side. They're on a high cliff looking down into a bay where ships are docking.

Chapter 3

Traveling around the central coast of California is almost impossible without a car or motorcycle. James had a Harley-Davidson chopper. He kept the bike under the back yard lemon tree, covered and protected by a heavy canvas tarpaulin. I was thinking that if I wanted to last or make it in this region I'd soon need my own transportation.

However, on the sunny morning we drove to Salinas, to finally begin our official business, thoughts of traveling and getting around weren't foremost in my mind. Of the two routes covering the twenty mile distance between coastal Monterey and inland Salinas, James took the more scenic one. There were green pastured ranches bordered by white fences along both sides of the road. Horses were meditatively grazing in the fields. Driving past the Laguna-Seca road race course James told me he has a friend that builds cars to race there. I watched a colt prancing through the morning cool, kicking up his heels in celebration of being alive.

The Spreckels sugar beet processing plant, approaching Salinas, produced a pungent vile odor as the land flattened into valley and the sea breezes were no more. All along the outskirts of the county seat lettuce fields were filled with stooping Mexican farm hands. The lettuce pickers were so low to the ground they seemed to be a different form of human life that hadn't straightened up yet. Their development as a race being retarded by being forced to bend for others. The workers were scattered near and far throughout the brown furrowed fields. Their traveling vehicles, mostly old station wagons, were parked along the sides of the dusty roads. The white bosses overseeing the shredding machines were busy counting loads of salad with clipboards in their hands. The child labor laws didn't seem to apply to Mexican children.

"We've got a lot of Chicanos at the high school," James said, as we drove along Alisal Street past the junior college, and then the Steinbeck Library.

"I've read some of his books," I responded to James' question. "But not that one. I've never even heard of it."

If you haven't read CANNERY ROW then you won't know anything about this country," he said. The difference between the arid inland farm community contrasted sharply with Monterey. It didn't seem as though they were both in the same county.

We drove through an unsmirched clean downtown. It didn't take very long. Then approaching some small mountains that limited our range I saw the modern facility, the high school. It was one of three in Salinas. The high school is the last building on Emlen Road on the northeast part of town. The neighborhood is residential. I had to get accustomed to the idea that a driver of a vehicle in California must stop for crossing pedestrians. Anyplace. It seemed like a pain in the neck after doing it a few times, because the youngsters, taking advantage of that rule, would wade out into traffic like they wanted to get run over, instead of waiting for a natural break in the flow.

Since classes hadn't started yet there were plenty of places to park. No congestion. I noticed a mob of students in front of the building. I thought they wished they could get in the doors and start learning.

As James and I walked past the crowd they started hollering

THERES NO VACATION FROM DESIRE

obscenities at us. In English that I could understand, and in Spanish, which I couldn't. James translated for me though. "When you work around here you learn Spanish as part of the job", my cousin told me.

A big plate glass window in front of the building was shattered, and James said, "It's the Mexican kids. They do this every year. They say they're not treated as well as the whites. I treat them all the same."

We walked through the campus grounds to get to the office. Upon asking, I was told my man was in and would see me in a few minutes. James had to go to work then and couldn't linger telling me what to do. After a brief wait in the bustling outer office I was asked to enter the inner room.

Mr. Sender was an effeminate man in his mid forties. He had the pallor of a drinker. He conducted himself professionally and treated me with respect and courtesy. His conservative suit and short, neatly parted hair fit his image.

Although he didn't refer to it I knew his main order of business was dealing with the racial conflicts outside, and he was pressed for time. He started talking immediately about the business we had to discuss. I sat the entire time I was in his office. He described the job to me, the opening, but from what he was saying I knew I didn't qualify, and that nothing I ever did before was like it. Before he finished talking about it and way before any conclusions had been reached I knew I wouldn't get it, and started my internal panic, wondering what my next step should be.

Even though I expected him to tell me the job didn't come into my realm of experience, I didn't actually think he would, but when he did, my greenness and lack of poise, caused my mouth to fly open, in addition to exhibiting the fear and terror that was in my eyes. Mr. Sender immediately saw my discomfort. He may have even thought I was on the verge of a tantrum or something. He began telling me, almost in the same breath that he couldn't hire me, about some of the other openings around town. Although that helped some, I still felt hopeless, and desperate for security.

In addition to his normal teaching duties James also had a light schedule of counseling. He told me the steps of decline of his own nervous breakdown were so vivid to him that he could recognize the process in others, and thought it was his responsibility to help the adolescent victims. I sprinted to the counseling quanset hut in back of the main building after my interview with Mr. Sender and James asked me for details on what was said and done and I told him.

"He wants me to go over to the Gray Eagle School now and talk with some guy over there," I continued.

"That's the place I started out at in this town," James winced. "You won't like it there, but a job's a job."

"What's wrong with it?" I asked him getting myself ready for another round of rejection.

"Straight-laced shitheads," James responded. "No room to move. They spy on everything you do. If it doesn't fit their pattern they give you heat. Makes you paranoid. Understand?"

"Yeah."

"The chief's all right. It's that backstabbing bastard assistant principal you have to watch out for. He coaches football too. He never played the game though. He was just an asshole do nothing jock living in the gym before he turned supervisor."

THERES NO VACATION FROM DESIRE

In James' counseling hut he had beanbag chairs arranged in a circle on a heavily green carpeted floor. The students could sprawl out as they talked about their problems. On the other side of a thin wall, in another teachers jurisdiction, were rows of industrial machines where problemed children trained to fit into society. James showed me the setup and said, "I advise out here twice a week. I teach logic and math inside to the smart ones, and then I come out here and teach survival to the nuts."

"I can't get away from the crazies," I was thinking, making the short trip to Gray Eagle after James had given me the key to his truck. From what he told me of the flat-topped coach-supervisor, whom he called "Kelly," and I didn't know if that was his first or last name, I was expecting the worst.

When I arrived at the place it seemed like classes had already begun. There were students all over the place looking glad to be getting back after their summer vacations.

The entire system seemed informal, the opposite of the way James told me they ran it there. Based on the information I'd received from my cousin I wasn't too sure if I even wanted this job. A lousy setup and the freedom to deal with it could be acceptable, but a bummer job without the autonomy to toil with it realistically is out. That was one of the main reasons I'd left My Guardian Angel school back East.

I found my way to the office and the first person I met was the Kelly that James had told me about. I discovered that was his last name, but everyone used it as though it was his first, but I called him Mr. Kelly. We spoke in the principal's office while the chief was out.

"What type of job were you told we have here?" Mr. Kelly asked, businesslike.

"Special Education."

"Yes, that's right. Can you tell me something about yourself that would qualify you for it?"

We started talking so fast and fluently and got the discussion moving so quickly that I didn't know if I should think of this an official interview.

"I taught that subject for one year in New York City."

"One year?", he seemed disappointed.

"Yes. I have strong letters from my supervisors there too", I said, starting to take the statement from Mr. Bowe from my jacket pocket, but Kelly responded by saying, "Save it".

"Do you feel able to work with the out of the ordinary?" he resumed.

"Yes sir," I said without hesitation.

As the conversation continued the principal walked in with a steaming cup of coffee in his hand. He was a slightly older man with a courteous demeanor. He was soft and flaccid, his left cheek hanging way lower than his right. I wondered if his shoe sizes matched.

I spoke with them both for a good fifteen minutes. When the discussion ended Mr. Kelly brought me out to another set of those inescapable quanset huts, the homes of the disabled, the homes of the boys and girls they don't want in their main building.

Mr. Kelly introduced me to a school marm old enough to be a great grandmother. She ruled the huts and was supposed to team teach with the

THERES NO VACATION FROM DESIRE

person the administration would hire. From what I could gather, she had the final say of who would be there working with her. I took an instant dislike to her, she reminding me of the clinicians at My Guardian Angel.

The children behaved both good and bad. They reacted to the same stimuli as city kids. It was obvious to the supervisors that after only a few minutes of interaction with the students I gained rapport with them, and could most likely handle the job. My only doubt was working with the old lady. She used heavy discipline to check them, instead of loving freedom to let them learn an little about themselves.

I spent about a half hour in the hut and returned to the main building with Mr. Kelly. We went to see the principal again. I felt good because I knew they were going to ask me when I could report for work. "Right now!", I was ready to blurt out.

I was comfortably seated with Mr. Kelly sitting to my right. We were both facing the principals desk. "We're beginning formal interviews for that position next week", the principal said. I already knew from my first disappointment that day to keep my mouth shut, no gaping, and to keep my eyes level and unemotional.

"We can pencil you in right now, Mr. Franklin. When are you available?"

"At your convenience," I responded, wishing he'd ink me in instead.

"How about the end of next week? Thursday? Is that all right?"

"Yes, Fine," I said, thinking my turn came at the end of the week, at the end of the roller coaster, at the end of the line, at the end of the world.

"So it's eleven thirty next Thursday," I confirmed, thinking they'd scheduled me close to lunch and they'd keep the interview short.

Before going to get James before returning to Monterey, I drove around the town for a half hour or so. There was a derelict section along the train tracks called Chinatown. It dates back to the time the China men built the railroad through Salinas. They didn't stick around. I didn't see one Chinaman in Chinatown. The adobe courthouses and jails were at the center of town.

It felt about ten times hotter here in the county seat than in Monterey. I could understand why James would live on the coast even though he told me he had to stand up to some pressure from influential townees to move to Salinas.

The counselor ended his day early. When I arrived with the truck he was ready to go , waiting near the cracked plate glass window that I saw this morning before my rejections. He hopped in on the passenger side saying, "You may as well get used to driving in the country, Jack. How'd things go over at the Gray Eagle?".

"Not bad," I said, excited, believing I'd scored. "They're having the formal talks next week. It looks like I can't do what they want me to do there."

"Who'd you talk with?"

"That Kelly you told me about. He didn't seem like such a bad guy."

"That's because you're not on the payroll yet. All he wants there are yes men. No one has any better ideas than him. I wrote a song about that sucker once, but threw it away after playing it on my drums.

THERES NO VACATION FROM DESIRE

"Why? Sound lousy?".

"I almost broke the damn skins I hit them so hard. That's why."

Hitting the edge of town, traveling west towards the coast again, James pointed to a roadside coffeehouse with trailer trucks parked around it. There was a big paved lot in back of the place where drivers could spend the night in their hammocks in their cabs. The variety of license plates represented at least half the states of the Union.

"Nah, it's kind of hot for coffee," I said, declining James' offer. "It looks crowded too."

"It usually is. Every trucker in the valley stops there. Most of them are hauling fruit and vegetables out to the other states."

Driving over an arching ridge in the road I heard a frightful roar coming up behind us. Through the rearview mirror I saw a riot of spotlights, and I heard James say "Oh shit" as thought he was expecting trouble.

"What's the matter?" I asked him, confused by the lights, the sound, and James' reaction.

"You'll know in about ten seconds partner." Within the amount of time he allotted there came next to me a mongrel who appeared to be a leftover of Genghis Kahns' boys. Instead of riding a horse he was driving a motorcycle. His Nazi helmet gave his politics away.

I took a closer look at the monstrosity wearing narrow slit sunglasses. He was cruising next to us along the dividing line of the two lane highway. He was giving me the finger, performing masturbatory gestures, and blowing kisses. The roar from the horde, only a few feet in back of us, sounded like something I never imagined.

I was mesmerized by the sight and sound surrounding us. The ape riding next to us lowered his acceleration and fell back again. The gang tailgated us so closely that if I'd stepped on the brakes some of them would've crashed into us.

"What the hell are these guys doing?", I said, starting to get excited, sensing I had to escape stepping on the accelerator, hearing James say, "It won't do you any good trying to outrun them, Jack."

"What are they? Angels?"

"Losers. The Angels scout them for members. The Angels are banned from the Monterey Peninsula. They're arrested on sight. Ever since they gang banged those girls at Monterey Pop."

People in cars going in the opposite direction slowed down and stared, but the bikers were on our case and didn't bother with anyone else. "Why don't they do something already?" I asked, becoming unnerved by their tactics.

"They might not do anything. I used to ride with them", James said modestly. "They hate me because I left them. They know my truck. Stay loose. Wish I had my headgear."

"Some friends", I moaned.

As soon as we saw the road sign informing us that Monterey was only five miles away, the bikers surrounded us and slowed down to fifteen miles an hour. Since I was in their midst I had to comply with their speed. James stayed calm, didn't panic, and said, "Go where they lead us. No use trying to bust out."

THERES NO VACATION FROM DESIRE

Pointing to an obese beast on a motorcycle with low tires, James said, "There's Lenny. He's the stupidest guy I've ever known. I saw that prick punch out an old guys' last tooth in the Surf Club one night."

"That's great," I said, rubbing my mouth. "Where are they taking us?"

"I don't know."

"What do they want from us?"

"I don't know."

"Where's the Highway Patrol?"

"Who knows."

Their membership was overpoweringly large. At least seventy bikes. Maybe a hundred. They were invincible. I gave up all thoughts of escape. I rode within the mobile mob going in the direction we were being led.

James wasn't afraid and that was the only thing that kept me calm. They held us captive along the road, leading us past Monterey to the adjacent town of Seaside, next to Ford Ord.

"They're taking us to the Flats in Seaside," James concluded. "The Blacks live there. The only others you see there are soldiers from the fort looking for drugs and sex."

We finally came to a stop in a dismal crumbling shanty town where the shacks and huts were permanent structures.

"Turn the fucking motor off," a voice snarled at me.

"Stay cool and let me do all the talking," James said. "This is Roy Johnsons' house. A damn filthy Okie. Don't hold your nose when they bring us in there no matter how bad it stinks."

And man, did it stink, with livestock and fighting cocks crowing around. Dogs and cats and chickens, manure piles, and a gummouthed blond haired human that weighed a ton and carried a billy club.

Most of the gang waited outside the dilapidated shack, but five or six of them were inside with us. They were drinking beer and whiskey, smoking joints, eating pills, scratching their balls, farting and belching. Good ole boys. We're having a party tonight.

"The boys said they saw your truck and decided to give you and escort," Roy said. His mountainous body moved towards me. He was six feet five inches or more. He said into my face, though talking to James, "Who's this cock sucker with the suit on?"

"Family. From back East," James responded as though we didn't have anything to worry about.

"Do it," Roy ordered one of his tribe. A simian faced small fry with massive arms and veins that bulged from working on machinery, approached me. I was stunned when I saw him take his clothes off. I could smell the foul rags from where they were on the floor.

"Now take yours off," he grinned. I was ready to fight if he'd told me to bend over.

Roy, taking in this scene, was stroking a cute pink piglet that was snorting and wheezing on the couch next to him. I was forced to exchange clothing with the biker who had taken his off. When I put the filthy greasy jeans on they seemed to be alive with vermin, and caked with shit and piss. I almost gagged.

Roy turned to James, after giving the pig a whack on the ass making it squeal and dart out the front door, and said to my cousin, "Why haven't you been buying from me? We know where you go. It's a small town here", Roy said to me. "Everyone knows everyone else's business."

"You know I can't be seen with you or any of The Losers. They'd bust me in a second," James replied.

"We can work something out," Roy said. "You want The Losers to break up for lack of money? If you buy anyplace else from now on you'll be getting another escort. And we'll take care of you then. The only reason I don't kick your fucking teeth down your throat now is because you used to be a Loser. That's the only thing that saved your ass. Now get the fuck out of here. Get what you want from Mitch. He's waiting outside."

"You too," the leader of the pack said to me. "Get out of here and if you need anything you'd better buy it from me."

"Yes," was all I could mutter, because I was holding my breath and couldn't wait to get into the truck where I could take the clothing off and fling them out the window.

While removing the clammy trousers and sweat soaked stinking shirt. James said, "There's a shovel in back of the truck. You should do the world a favor and bury those things". I was in no mood for jokes.

"Too late now," I said, heaving them out, breathing in some clean fresh air, continuing, "Lets' roll the windows up and put the AC on."

He accommodated me, but after a few minutes it felt very cold and I got goose bumps, complained about it and James replied, "That's what you get for riding around in your jockies."

"Well it sure as hell isn't my fault," I began raising my voice, not caring if I offended him, not caring if he went for the rifle, ready to make him eat it if her threatened me with it again. "You and your crummy fucking drugs! Can't you do without that shit? They stole my best suit and left me stinking like a skunk just because you don't spend your fucking money on their stuff."

"Now hold on there," James almost shouted.

Before he had a chance to finish his sentence I said, "Now how the hell do I get in the house without wearing any pants? The neighbors will think I'm a fucking nut like you. You're more nuts than smart. Lousy drugs. Can't you do without them?".

"No I can't!" he bellowed back at me, lowering his eyes, embarrassed by his weakness. "And if I wasn't in slow motion with the stuff right now I'd throw you out the fucking door instead of listening to your shit". Before another word was spoken he drew back his fist and punched me in the cheek. My head snapped back. When I recovered I returned his punch. The truck went out of control. We veered into a roadside ditch, and by some miracle the momentum carried us back out onto the road again. We came to a stop.

"Right here," I shouted, jumping out onto the road wearing nothing but my Fruit Of The Looms, putting my fists up. "Bring that rifle out here!" I ordered James. "I want to shove it up your ass! You get me involved with the scum of the earth! You'll pay for it now!"

"Yes sir," James said, jumping out of the truck with his first step and jumping on my head with his second. We began wrestling and punching each other hard. After a few minutes of this brutality it was getting obvious that we were getting to like each other. Slowly, the blows turned to laughs.

When all the gruesome pent up tensions had been released we stood there laughing and laughing. James finally said, "You better get your ass back in the truck before they arrest you for indecency." Before I got in though I made him promise to buy me a new pair of pants on the way home, since he had a job and I didn't.

Chapter 4

On Thursday I had to take the bus to Salinas because James left early in the morning for his job. Too early for me to go with him. However, I decided to hitchhike thinking it would be quicker than the bus. Wearing a suit, almost as good as the one The Losers stole from me, I was on the road with my thumb out looking for a ride.

After baking on the pavement for a half hour or so I was beginning to become concerned about not only arriving on time for my interview, but the shape my clothing would be in by the time I got there. It was a dusty road to say the least. My dark suit was showing all the specks already. I was thinking that maybe I should've taken the bus.

Fortunately, a newly painted hot rod stopped for me within a few minutes. When I saw the driver looking just like a Loser I thought I'd better not get in. Sure enough, as I was entering the big car I saw the denim jacket of the motorcycle gang draped across the front seat.

The interior of the GTO was gutted. It didn't have any extras, not even a radio. The bearded biker driving his car was telling me about life on the Central Coast after discovering I was a newcomer to the area and was looking for a job.

"Good luck," he said. "I've been looking for work around here for five years and haven't come up with anything yet. I just have to make a few dollars when I can. I'm building a race care right now. I've got a good chance of winning some prize money at Laguna-Seca in a few weeks. You should come out. That's a good way of finding out what's going on around here."

"Maybe I will," I told him, almost mentioning James' name, but thinking if I did it might upset the balance and pleasant mood of the biker. "I've only been out here about a month now. I've had a few leads, but nothing much has happened."

"What do you do?" he asked.

"I'm a teacher."

He was speeding, but when he heard what my occupation was he skidded to a dead stop. He pulled up on the side of the road and said to me looking at the door handle on my side of the car, "See that?" His personality change was so abrupt and unforeseen that I didn't know what was going on. After being exposed to the Loser lifestyle, and knowing what that breed was capable of once riled, I said, "See what?", very peacefully.

"The handle, fucker," he said belligerently.

"Yeah."

"Use it. Get out!"

Not bothering to learn about his difficulties with authority figures in the past I opened the door, got out, and stood on the blacktop with my thumb out waiting for another ride. Within moments a station wagon with a Mexican family in it stopped. The driver, a small man, perhaps thirty-five years old, told me he was on his way to Salinas, and if that was my destination, jump in. I sat on the back seat with his two little girls. His wife kept a steady gaze out the front window never looking back at me. The driver seemed like the only one who could speak English. He was very friendly.

"You looked mucho important with those clothes on, señor," he said curious.

"I'm a working man like you. I'm looking for work now. These are my best clothes."

"Ah señor," he smiled, "I have my clothes for looking too."

The girls in the back with me were very shy, and didn't even move for a few minutes. When they saw their father and I were getting along they began giggling and carrying on. They finally had to be silenced by their mother who raised her voice to them speaking Spanish. I don't know what she said but the girls calmed down. One of them was tired and before long she fell asleep with her head on my shoulder.

"We just came up from the border," the gentleman said. "We've got a job here picking lettuce. I come North every year for this. Good boss man. You need a job? You want to work the fields?"

"It may come to that soon," I said, "but I have something else to check out first."

"You'll get it," he guaranteed me.

"My brother, he lives in Salinas all year. His boy goes to job training. Keeps him out of the fields. My little girls," who were both tired and sleeping now, "help me outside. Maybe someday I hope they learn other jobs too. No picking. Bad back," he said, reaching around to his lower back to illustrate his point, complaining about one of his occupational hazards.

"Yes, my brothers' boy. We're very proud of him. He goes to the big learning center in Salinas. Accounting and bookkeeping. Work inside. Out of the sun."

"In Salinas you said?"

"Si. He goes to school downtown. He's very smart. A genius with numbers. The school is big and many of my people go there. He gets a stipend from the American government. Maybe someday my girls can go," he dreamed. "No fields for them," he concluded.

His wife turned around and she was so burnt wrinkled brown from the sun she appeared to be an old lady. But when she smiled offering me an apple I saw she had the face of a girl too, and couldn't have been more than twenty-eight.
"Thank you," I said, taking her offering, waking the girls.
"My brother," the driver continued, "We're going to his house now. We start work tomorrow, I hope. His boy will be at The Jobs' Congress learning how to work the books," he smiled, thinking of his familys' upward mobility.

We spent our words and were mostly silent for the remainder of the short ride into Salinas. When we saw the workers in the fields he noticed some faces he hadn't seen since last year that made him happy. They left me off in the heart of downtown, about two miles from the Gray Eagle.

After finding out that public transportation was virtually nonexistent I decided to walk the distance to the part of town I needed. I still had over an hour before the interview started. Also, I was tense, and I knew walking would relax me, and that by the time the talking started I'd be loose and ready for anything that may happen.

While rambling along the sunny streets with adobe and ranch houses, lawns and affluence, I sensed I was being followed by a car. Then I heard, "Hey Peppy! Hey hot sauce!" They can't be talking to me I thought and continued walking. I moved to the center of the sidewalk instead of staying near the curb.

THERES NO VACATION FROM DESIRE

When the torrent of racial abuse pouring from the mouths of the inhabitants of a green reconditioned fifty-eight Chevy continued, I finally took a long look through the windshield to see who had classified me as an enemy.

"We don't want you here. Got your papers Peppy?" the boy closest to me said, leaning back, sinking into the comfortable interior upholstery. The driver was sun burnt with long hair parted in the middle. They were teenagers.

I reversed myself and began walking back in the opposite direction, hoping to lose them. They made a U turn and followed me from the far side of the street, talking louder. I turned and started walking my original route again. They made a U turn and continued to dog me. They drove along the curb. They were only a few feet away from me.

As I walked straight ahead, crossing a street, an object hit my shoulder causing me to take a stagger step forward. I took the apple from my pocket that the Mexican woman had given me, spun, and flung it at the glaze eyed teenager. The fruit hit his chin so hard it splattered into instant cider. He was out cold. His arms were dangling limp from the window.

I proceeded walking very slowly scanning the ground for other weapons. The town was so clean though, that there was no refuse or rocks in the street to defend myself with. I decided, if the driver continued following me, which it seemed he wasn't I was ready to holler for help.

On my last look back the long haired driver was trying to revive the loud mouth passenger by pouring beer between his lips. Where am

I? Going to an interview I remembered. When I started thinking about the questions the educators could ask I could only think about what had just happened to me. I was hoping that my blank concerning educational theory world return and the reality of the streets would be gone soon.

Within sight of my destination a police car hopped the curb in front of me. An officer leaped out, saying, "We hear you've been causing trouble." Before I had a chance to say anything he grabbed me by my tie, ripping off one of the button down tabs on my collar, and flung me against the front fender of the squad car. My hands were spread over the engine hood which was red hot. The officers' hatless partner had his hand on his holstered pistol.

When I offered no resistance the law cooled out. He asked me to turn around, and said, bewildered, "You're not Mexican?"

"Never have been either," I responded, not trying to be funny.

"We just got a complaint a person dressed like you walking in your direction was throwing objects at moving vehicles trying to cause accidents. The report said you were Mexican."

"I'm not. I didn't start any trouble either," I said respectfully, telling myself I'd tell them the facts and that should clear me.

"New York? What the hell are you doing walking these streets, mister," he asked, peering out from under his wide brimmed soft hat, studying my identification. I explained to him why I was where I was and how I got there and what had happened a few minutes ago.

"You made yourself some enemies, Mr. Franklin."

"I don't worry about people who hate me because of my looks. There's nothing I can do about it anyway."

"You're right," he said, friendly like, "but we have these racial

THERES NO VACATION FROM DESIRE

incidents out here every so often. If you're not white, especially in this part of town, the kids make it hard on you. You know", he continued, "from a certain angle, Mr. Franklin, it's easy to mistake you for something you're not."

The car with my tormentors arrived, and both bigots raved, "That's him! He's the one!" I felt safe with the law there now. They knew the truth. I felt free to take a lengthily combative look at my enemies so I'd be able to know them in the future if need be. There wasn't anything unusual or outstanding or conspicuous about their appearance that would help me to remember them. Just two dull and common faces.

"We want to make a complaint," they whined to the presiding officer, causing the other policeman to join the discussion.

"This man's not Mexican," the cop retorted, not wanting an ugly scene to get any worse. "You said he was Mexican. You can see for yourself he's the same as you, and not an illegal alien. He was born and raised here in the USA. If you boys know what's good for you you'd better let this whole thing drop."

The narrow minded racists were persistent in wanting to get their own way like spoiled affluent children. They insisted they wanted to file a complaint against me because the kid thought his jaw was broken and it might've been, it was swelled out so far. So I got a free ride in the squad car to almost the same spot downtown where the Mexican field hands left me off, and where I started walking from. I looked at my watch and saw that my job interview started eight minutes ago.

The desk sergeant listened to the patrol car cop for details, then told me I could file a counter compliant to protect myself. Although I didn't want to go to court or get involved in any legal proceedings, if this was my only defense I'd have to use it. Once the intolerant townees realized I could make life miserable for them too, they seemed to change their minds. Before long they were hinting they didn't want to get involved either.

While walking back to the highway, looking for a ride to Monterey, I took my suit jacket off because it was so hot out. As I flung it over my shoulder I noticed a small rip where the boy had hit me in the shoulder with his projectile. Of course, where the tab collar button had been torn off my shirt by the cop was a big gap now. I'd better stop wearing such good duds out here in beautiful California.

Two very old boys or very young men eased to a stop for me. They had a big purple van, and the one on the passenger side asked, wearing a timid, withered smile, "you going towards the coast?"
"Yeah."
"We can take you most of the way."
The interior of the vehicle reeked of a mixture of incense and pot.

The van was big enough to be a home on wheels. It was carpeted silver. Very thick and comfortable to sit on. There were hidden musical speakers all over. I didn't care for the disco tape playing though. At first they didn't say anything as I was getting used to it in the back among their multitude of garden tools and empty fertilizer sacks.
"We're going to the Monterey Airport," the one who had done all the talking continued. "We can let you off there."
It was a good ride and all I said was "Thank you."

"You don't sound like you're from here?" the driver casually asked, with a nonregional feminine lisp.

"No. I'm an Easterner. From New York City. I'm looking for work out here."

"You'll need luck, stranger," the driver continued.

"We're from D. C. The Capital." His partner said, "Roll up the window. I want to turn the AC on." The blast of cold air felt great.

"We've only been out here a year," Clark said, the passenger, who introduced himself and his partner, Ron. "We've been doing carpentry and gardening since we got here. We left office jobs back in Washington. Important work too. Here, take a look at this", and he shoved a huge looseleaf notebook into my hands. I scanned the book for information, but the language was so technical it was meaningless to me.

"It must've paid a lot," I said.

"And how. But we're much happier out here now. Monterey is such a beautiful town. We have a cottage near Cannery Row. You must come and visit us sometime. Do you have any friends out here?"

"Sure. Plenty."

They lit up a joint. When they asked me if I wanted some I took a hit. Contemplating I could buy from them and stay away from the dangerous Losers, I asked, "Do you know where I could get some? I'm looking for new connections."

"We've got plenty," Clark said, Ron remaining mute ever since he said his few words. They gave me there telephone number and address and told me when I'm running low they could provide the weed.

They turned in off the highway onto a narrow road that led into the airport. They stopped at a small read and white checkered tool shed, and put some utensils from their van in it. In return they took more tools from the shed and put them in the van.

"We finished building a sundeck this morning in Carmel Valley. Now we have a gardening job to go to. We have to switch our tools. We're going back in the direction we just came from," Ron said. They left me off very close to town and it was easy getting home from there.

I arrived at my house in a state so dissipated if I'd had dogs they wouldn't have recognized me. Climbing the back steps that led to our common sundeck porch, Ralph was in his usual place. He was sitting in a comfortable beach chair while sipping from a can of beer. There was a silver cooler next to him. He saw my raggedness and said, "You'd never last in The Corps with that look, hang dog". For a guy who knew he was going to die soon he was very tranquil. He didn't get excited about anything. He was wonderful company.

He had a rare muscle disorder caused by a tropical disease he caught in the Philippines during his last year of active service. He was a flabby, loose limbed forty-five year old wearing a khaki tank top t-shirt. He was balding in patches from the disease. His condition also caused him to be constantly squint eyed, and had to wear very dark sunglasses all the time.

"Don't tell me your troubles," he warned, handing me a beer from the cooler, "unless you tell it funny, or unless it has a sadder ending than mine." He joked about his premature demise. Although in a worse condition than ever since I'd been using up my money, Ralph always got me to relax and to enjoy the moment.

With the late afternoon sunshine pouring down on us, Ralph said,

"I'm glad that crazy son of a bitch cousin of yours started working again. Now I can sit out here all day and dream about going to heaven without hearing those drums."

"He told me you like them?"

"Sometimes. But that boy is geared for combat all the time. I've had my share of that drum and fighting stuff. But I've been around men like James all my life and it don't bother me. I like guys like him. I'd rather be around that type if I have any choice. If I didn't hear him pounding those drums in there I'd ask him what's wrong."

"How about another tall one?" he asked through his gritty always present smile caused by his squinting.

"Okay."

"Coolers' empty," Ralph said, rising from the beach chair. His coordination was starting to go, and he walked with a semistoop and shuffling gate.

"It'll just be a matter of time before I'm getting around like a God damned two hundred pound baby", he said. "I won't even be able to drive soon. It's kind of interesting watching my body fall apart while my mind is still sharp. Come here," he ordered me. "I want to show you something inside."

Entering Ralph's apartment it was the mirror image of mine next door. He scrambled to the refrigerator taking out a six pack to bring outside. He put it on the table and went into another room. While he was gone I scanned the kitchen. It looked like his Japanese girlfriend kept it in good order, it was so neat and clean.

There was an odd calendar on the wall. It was homemade, custom made, with its' own marking, though finalized by a professions printer. It had the months right, but the days were backwards, making it a countdown of some sort. The days were marked off with X's indicating the amount of time he had left.

Ralph entered the room with a solid black package that looked like cufflinks and a tie clip could be in it. When in front of me he opened the lid and said, "Did you ever see the Congressional Medal Of Honor before?"

"No," I said impressed, knowing the great deeds and sufferings that earns such a trophy. "Is it yours'?"

"It sure is, boy," his southern accent rising to the top.

"I was the best shot in my unit. My eyes are gone now. But I could see like an eagle then. I was a sniper among other things. I got this for acts of bravery," he laughed. "In Korea. It's all written out in official language on that citation in there. Someday I'll let you read it. I just don't like to talk about the dead. But I'm more proud of that medal than anything else in my life, including my sweet woman. But don't tell her that," he chuckled.

He was getting loose and atrophied from all his sitting and guzzling, and as he was telling me his story he was sweating heavily, as though he were imagining himself under enemy fire again. "Korea. Damn hell hole. A lot of buddies went down there. After that even dying is easy."

We started to go onto the back sundeck again, but before we went out I asked him about the backwards calendar. What was it for. I'd never seen one like it before. I thought it might be some kind of military calendar.

"Oh that thing?" he said. "That's my countdown to what you may call disaster, but what I call bliss. I believe in The Bible. I have no doubt I'm going home to a loving God and a loving family. So I'm counting the days until I die. I'm lucky I know when I'm going. It's an advantage. Some may not think so, but I sure do. It takes all the pressure off."

"I never knew what I wanted until I learned I was going to die young," Ralph continued. "Then I figured out I didn't want anything. I love to do nothing. It seems like the real purpose of life. Doing nothing is doing something. It's not idleness. I'm doing what I want to do."

"I was one hell of a gung ho Marine too," the combat veteran went on. "When I found out and faced the truth I started living in accordance with it. Work and toiling for money had nothing to do with living a useful life. All money is fool's gold."

"But isn't it depressing looking forward to dying?" I asked.

"Life's ultimate goal is looking ahead to dying. Not fearing it."

The discussion saddened me knowing such a good man would be gone soon. I excused myself after sitting outside with Ralph for awhile. I drank another beer from my refrigerator, and sat at James' drums trying to come up with some type of rhythm. But the instrument was so big and complex I should've been hitting the little rubber pad instead. However, I discovered if I only stayed on one drum, either the tomtom or the snare, I could produce my own soothing beat.

James arrived as I was checking out the cymbals and said, "How come you didn't show up for your interview today?"

He was so belligerent and bullish he set me off again, and I said, "What's it to you?"

"What's it to me?" he asked, stunned by my arrogance, "what's it to me? Who got you in to talk with all those people? Who's name and reputation have you been living off since you got here? Who's been trying to help you score, and who has to see those people you fucked every day?"

"Who?" I asked, watching him kick one of his bass drums, though not hard enough to break it.

"Sender called me in his office today and told me he got a call from Kelly over at Gray Eagle. Then he gave me the pleasant news that you didn't even show up. You know where that leaves me? You should be coming to me for counseling."

"I know. I know," I said, starting to apologize, realizing the embarrassing position I put him in. "But I've got a good excuse."

So I told him the entire story and he listened intently. It was an odd thing too. Now that all my chances for a job were shot I didn't feel the pressure much at all. I was in fact, relieved. I even wanted to celebrate. What, I didn't know.

James was not angry after hearing what I went through that day.

"It's a shame that had to happen," he said.

"Why? They wouldn't have hired me anyway. I knew that all along."

"That's where you're wrong, buddy. They were all set to take you on. They had been asking about you. Both Sender and I were asked questions about you this morning. They like you and thought you could help them."

"I'd better phone them tomorrow," I said.

"It won't do you any good anymore. You didn't even bother getting in touch with them, and they don't want to deal with people like that. Your chances of working in this county are over. They wouldn't take you now if you were the only one left. Don't expect me to help you out now. I've done everything I could. You loused yourself up and don't have anyone

THERES NO VACATION FROM DESIRE

to blame but yourself. You're blacklisted. You may as well move. No chance of working around here."

Chapter 5

I finally had to admit to myself, based on the lack of love from the letters going between Lena and I, that our relationship was fading. There was little to hold out for. Her messages were getting shorter and shorter and less loving. The worst part was that my letters to her were turning out the same way. We were losing interest in each other.

My body was beginning to ache. My mind was beginning to erode taking a forced vacation from desire. The quality of my life was degenerating because of a severe deprivation of love. The choice was mine, and I seemed to be making it. The complexity of enduring a state of breakdown was confusing me. The demand on my powers, channeling them into subhuman survival activity was wasting me.

"It sounds like that girl don't love you as much as you thought," James said with the overindulgence of compassion he'd learned from advising adrift youngsters.
"You wouldn't say that if you knew her."
"Just the fact that you wanted me to read this letter tells me you need a lot of help with this, Jack. Did you see that little part at the end where she thanks you for the most wonderful year of her life?"
"Sure I read it," wanting to suppress it..
"It sounds like she's signing off there, Jack," brutally understating the thought I wanted no part of.
"She's letting you know in a subtle way she needs some loving," James continued with his nerve jagging, soft spoken, thought out analysis. "But we agreed it was all right for us to sleep with others. There's nothing wrong with that."

"You're not doing it. Are you?"

"No. But you can't prove she is either."

"No. Catch her attitude though. That's more important than the words. You and your girl may have a different set of values is all I'm saying. Don't kid yourself. If you loved her you'd still be there with her instead of being on the brink of collapsing and not knowing what to think or how to get along in the world. You hear what I'm saying?"

"Yeah. Loud and clear," but the ideas were so outrageous and true that I couldn't accept them, and reached for the drugs again. I was in no hurry to reach any conclusions.

Although I hadn't lined up anything for myself as my money dwindled and my prospects dimmed, I was way past the point of no return. I was pondering staying in Monterey getting any type of work I could. I spent most of my time roaming around town, stoned, trying to maintain my sanity.

The Coast Guard Wharf, the third major pier in town, juts into the bay just before you approach Cannery Row, coming from deep tourist Monterey of restaurants and gift shops, and Fisherman's Wharf. Although not many tourist venture onto the Coast Guard Wharf, it has its own attraction too. Sea life.

The Coast Guard Wharf is a big strong wide concrete pier that's opened to the public to walk on. The far tip of the structure is fenced off with chain link, because the sea lions congregate there. It's their place. Those huge, luminescent, whiskered creatures. They loll and relax on the hot concrete deck after going for a swim, maybe gliding under Fisherman's Wharf scarfing up some abalone.

THERES NO VACATION FROM DESIRE

They looked like walrus. The bulls must've weighed a ton. There was a series of rocks and boulders where they loafed and bellowed like a herd in the wild, which is what they were. At close range they looked friendly enough to bring home, but you'd need one hell of a tub.

I usually made my walking rounds while James played his drums. Some nights I listened to him and was so exhilarated by the live thundering beat he kept to the hard rock music on the stereo that I wouldn't even need as much smoke to cool out.

James played with the power, and it was good for all who listened. The medicine of the rhythm. The beat of the universe. The sound of singing man. The part time death of brooding beasts.

James created the cadences "Sunrise" and "Sunset" from feelings he experienced at Asilomar Beach. He set the world his own tune. He controlled without taking, stealing or pillaging. He clashed cymbals and rumbled drums. He brought me out with him to see and to feel. He was the genius of interpreting the worlds' phenomena, compressing it through his senses and sending it out again with music. I listened to the melody and drums, and saw Asilomar.

Just beyond Lovers Point there is nothing but a road and beach that's been left in its natural state. You park on the side of the blacktop on sand that's been hardened from the constant use of the natives of the peninsula. The road winds around and through many of the beach houses that exist there.

The beach itself is long and wide, and the sand is white. Since the surface is never cleaned or sifted there is always a kaleidoscopic variety of deep sea samples and other treasures that washed up on shore. If you don't want to sit on the sand you can sprawl on one of the enormous boulders that are scattered about.

At dusk you could see the big pink sun sink into the Pacific. Some nights she was red though. She gave the appearance that she was so close you could touch her if you reached out. It was hard to believe that something that close was so far away. Greatest illusion ever. You didn't need a slick magician to pull it off either. It's the oldest trick in the book.

All along the beach there's great viewing. You don't have to bunch with others to enjoy the mystical miracle, the orderly due death of light that takes place every night. "Morning has broken like the first morn," the song goes. She still goes down just like the first time too.

Cars and trucks are lined up along the road with the inhabitants waiting breathlessly and silently for the eternal spectacle to begin. Many lovers come to kiss, and the submerging sun is a sideshow for them. Most people parked their cars and walked out onto the beach so they could get even closer. It happened every night.

It seemed like it was the quietest time of the day too, at the conclusion. Oh Lord, we thank you for the blessing of another day. The only thing out there past the beach was the flat surface of the Pacific, the calm one, and the still waters looked inviting as the sun took her dip.

So big, so close, wondering what was holding her up. She sank lower and lower in the sky. The bottom of the burning ball would touch the top of the ocean's surface, and she looked like she was floating for a few seconds.

It's the only time of the day you can look at her without hurting your eyes. I'm glad I'll die before the sun, the life, burns out. One of the things that adds to the beauty of the setting sun is that the sight itself is so fleeting. She was gone so fast that it took the quality of investigation away from it. You had to view the scene as though it was a once in a life time occurrence.

Ralph stuck his head in through the kitchen door walking in off the sundeck, and said, "You Joes' know what time it is? What the hell is going on in here?" James was beating the drums and bobbing his head lost in the place wherever he was at the moment.

"Hey! Hey! Hey!" I hollered at the drummer boy, but to no avail as he continued hammering out his message and couldn't be interrupted. "Wake up James!" I hollered, but still no response from the artist.

"That boy's gone," Ralph grinned, amazed at the spectacle of the mad drummer. "He ain't never coming back. Where is he now? I wish he'd be quiet. My woman has to rise at dawn. She's been trying to set all night, but the drums are stirring her."

"Hey James!" I yelled once more at the rabid musician as he hit nonstop. After coming to an agreement with Ralph we doused James with a pitcher full of water, and he finally broke his revery and was among the living again.

"How'd it sound?" he inquired, instead of asking who dumped on him. "Loud boy," Ralph said. "My little woman is trying to relax. Give her a break, will ya?"

"I'm sorry, Ralph. I won't bother her again."

Chapter 6

I was at the stage where the old dream had just about broken down, and still too humbled at my lack of any good luck at all to start forming any new plans. It was a great relief to hear the Cream version of BORN UNDER A BAD SIGN running through my mind. I still wanted the old plans to work out. Negative momentum was the only thing carrying me along. "If it wasn't for bad luck I wouldn't have no luck at all," I could hear Jack Bruce singing, keeping me company. I'd followed up numerous leads, but they all went up in smoke.

I remember once, in the early morning, driving somewhere with my cousin through the sandy Fort Ord section, in a band of muffled sunshine. James, wearing his face visor sombrero, said to me, "I just want you to try one more guy before you go." I knew I would be leaving soon, hoboing to who know where, homeless, but as a last resort, as a favor to myself, I'd go see one more person.

"All right. One more guy," I said, the pressure off, since I didn't have to get a job here anymore, and could drift and escape from everything. Except myself.

Arriving in Salinas that same night, at the Gray Eagle School, I said to James, "This place looks familiar. I think I tried it already."

"Not the night shift".

"Night shift?"

"Yeah. The Adult School."

"Adult School?"

"Yeah. Here's the story. The person I'm taking you to see is in charge of the program. A lot of Spanish is spoken. Can you speak it?"

"Not a word", I said, relieved. "So I guess that leaves this out. Now I can go."

"Not so fast. They do a lot of other things too. They're a regular part of the public school system. Full salary and benefits. They set up shop when they can assemble enough students to make it legitimate."

"They had a school out at the county jail awhile back. A high school equivalency program."

"No more?"

"No. They went through five teachers in one year. They couldn't find anyone who could handle the cons. The last guy they had there got pasted out of the room with spitballs."

"What the hell are you getting me into? Jail?"

"No. I already told you they shut that place up. At Gray Eagle here they've had the language classes going on for fifteen years. They have a main building downtown where they base most of their classes. You're best chance now of staying here and bringing Lena out is working with these people. They're well respected and can only hire certified teachers. You hear me?"

"Keep talking."

"I'm friends' with the guy in charge of the entire setup. Sweetest guy in the world. The Adult School has its own principal in the district office, but the guy I'm taking you to see runs the whole show on a daily basis. He knows everything. He's originally form Cleveland. If he's got something he might be able to help you."

The Gray Eagle was a lot different at night than during the day. The atmosphere was much more mellow. James knew every teacher in every room as we went past. Most of them took the time to wave or say "Hello." Most of the students looked to be Mexicans, younger ones, in their late teens and early twenties. Not hunchbacked to the lettuce yet.

Walking along a green corridor with a few painting on the walls, approaching the room of our destination, we could hear an argument coming from within it. It was so loud we thought it was a violent free for all. Before we got to the doorway, a tall man, well dressed, and with a mustache, walked out of the room and left in the opposite direction. He took the time to straighten up a lopsided portrait of John Steinbeck that was hanging on the wall. He didn't see us.

Then entering the room he just left from I spied a stout man, fleshy about the jowls, holding a book with the corner missing, as though he'd just taken a bite out of it. Is this the sweetest guy in the world, I thought.

The violent incident was immediately repressed. No one mentioned it. The heavy set man put his hand out for James to shake. Just as we were about to say something to him, the telephone on his desk rang. He spun to answer it, and as he restrained his conversation, he put his index finger up to us finishing his greeting, indicating he was glad to see James, and just had to take the telephone call first.

He was a young man, in his early thirties, and obese to the point of being unhealthy. His clothing was casual, neat and clean. He conducted himself in such a professional way that he demanded a natural respect as someone who knew what he was doing. His little bit of city wariness left in him from Cleveland, made him seem more communicable to me. The fact that he was in charge of what could be called the oddball division of a legitimate school system added to his stature.

"Yes. Yes," he said into the telephone receiver, "we can supply you with a classroom if you have enough students. You have twenty-two! That's two to spare. And you have all your own equipment and gear? Excellent. If you can come in to see me sometime this week I can make all the arrangements. We needed and wanted a class in photography. I'll bet when some of the students here see your class you'll get them signing up too. Thank you. Yes. Nice talking with you. See you soon." I couldn't believe this gentle man was the screaming book eating savage of a few moments ago.

James introduced us. His eyes were twinkling now with the thought of expanding his program with a new photography class. He put his hand out to meet mine. He told me to take a seat.

The office was opened for all reasons, and teachers and students were constantly walking in helping themselves to workbooks and other materials from the cabinets and shelves. With each person he spoke with , Mr. Getz, whom everyone called Bill, shifted easily between English and Spanish as though they were one language. He seemed like a real smart guy. James said he'd be back in a few minutes and left us alone.

In between the never ending interruptions, Bill asked me a few questions about my background, and what type of work I'd done. As we spoke his eyes were flashing enthusiastically as he was trying to come up with something for me. He was wearing a green sports shirt with a little gold contribution pin in the collar indicating he was a supporter of the Salinas farm team of the San Francisco Giants.

After satisfying himself with his ordinary test, Bill asked, "Do you speak Spanish?"

"No."

"That's too bad. We need a teacher here right now. You could've started tomorrow night." He was soft spoken and wasn't trying to shock me with authority.

"Yes, Mr. Franklin," Bill continued. "A teacher with your background I'm sure would fit nicely into our system. If we have a choice we try to hire self motivated people. People who work well by themselves and don't need much supervision or instruction. People who can develop their own methods and improvise as things change. But there's nothing I can do for you right now as much as I'd like to. Did you ever think of starting your own class in something? If you can get twenty students together for any reason we could get it certified and get you a room right here. Salary, of course."

"No. I don't specialize in anything."

The conversation continued, and along with his constantly sparkling eyes, his gracious smile made me feel at home. "There's a job I know of in Salinas, Mr. Franklin. It might be something you may not want though."

"What is it?" I asked.

"It's not with us you must understand. Did you ever hear of the Jobs Congress? It's on Main Street. Downtown."

Recalling my hitchhiking ride with the Mexican family, I said, "Yes. I've heard of it."

"We have language classes established in their program. One of my teachers there told me the Jobs Congress needs someone for their General Education program. Teaching mostly field workers anything practical they need to know." Things started looking better.

We began to conspire, as Bill said, "The Director of Jobs Congress is Juan Soto. You must not tell him I sent you. He wouldn't hire you if he knew I sent you." I started wondering what all this murky business was about. I was speculating if I wanted to deceive a man to get a job. But I was as desperate as Tom Joad to find work.

When Bill saw I was interested despite the secrecy, he continued. "We have a history of stealing personnel away from their program," he grinned. "We've done it enough times now that the relationship between the Jobs Congress and the Adult School is an adversarial one. It's too bad. The field we're in you'd think we could cooperate more, but we're competing for students and money too. They need our language program in their school so they can continue getting government monies. So when you see Mr. Soto don't tell him I was the one who sent you."

With my involvement in the plot it seemed like I was already working for Bill. He was keeping me in a safe place until something finally opened up at the Adult School. The intrigue also made us fast friends. We talked and laughed as Bill continued to fill me in about the situation.

The Jobs Congress building wasn't very impressive looking. It seemed to be a large one level white washed converted garage or factory. The front wall had been removed and replaced by a huge plate glass window. I glanced in through the window before entering the building for the first time, and saw a horde of people milling about the soda and candy machines in the front lobby.

Entering through a side door, passing the junk food machines, I approached a receptionists' desk that fronted the faculty mailboxes. I spoke to a redheaded Spanish woman seated behind the desk, and said, "I'd like to see Juan Soto."

THERES NO VACATION FROM DESIRE

Mr. Soto was standing nearby among the crowd, and when he heard his name mentioned he approached me and introduced himself. He was tall and handsome with well defined Latin features including dark wavy hair. His face wasn't distorted in anger though, the way it was when leaving Bill Getz' office at Gray Eagle last night. I wondered if he ate books too. His eyes were large and every sad as though he were burdened with too many problems to handle. On first impression he seemed like a very nice man.

I was dressed well and had an envelope full of credentials with me for anyone who wanted to see them. I told Mr. Soto I heard there was a job opening there, and that I was applying for it. His cheerless eyes awakened. He put a friendly hand on my shoulder.

I understood right away from the serious way he was questioning me and sizing me up he was in need of a teacher. His bearing told me all this. His manner of speech and movement was very slow and sincere. He weighted everything he said before he said it, just like a politician. His soft spoken demeanor put me at ease with him. The fact that it was Columbus Day had no effect on the school schedule there.

He inspected my papers apparently making his decision as we stood in the lobby, which was now cleared of students who had returned to their classes. There was no doubt in my mind I'd get the job unless there was some technical issue involved. It was a private institution and didn't come under teacher state certification scrutiny, also meaning it didn't pay the good salaries. Mr. Soto apologized for only being able to offer me the minimum wage.

I thought Mr. Soto a decent man, and felt a little guilty not telling him how I found out about the job. Before I knew it, although he had to leave the building soon, he was showing me around the converted factory schoolhouse and pointing out some of the features of the job training program.

His office was immediately off the main lobby. It was a plain and simple room with a few business chart graphs on the wall. His charts indicated the growth and profits of the institution, rather than the personal development of human beings. A shelf over and behind his desk held knickknacks and small "cute" statues of elfish figurines of the "World's Greatest" variety. He told me he collects them.

Extending back off the lobby, after walking out of Mr. Sotos' office, were two corridors lined with classrooms. At the end of one of the corridors the building opened up into a very large classroom.

It was filled with typewriting students. Looking in, seeing how the program worked, the typewriters were in chorus, tapping out their daily secretarial blues, and the quick brown fox was scheming in the bushes. Mr. Soto wanted me to teach a class in general education. Basic arithmetic and English. A universal class for a common teacher. A good learning opportunity for me.

"That guy's heavy into politics," James said, tapping out a new song on the rubber pad.

"Nothing wrong with that, is there?"

"No, not really. It goes with the job he has. The Jobs Congress is more political than educational."

THERES NO VACATION FROM DESIRE

"I'll be in the classroom teaching. He never told me about politics."

"I just wanted you to know that Soto is deep into politics and people say he's Director of Jobs Congress just so he can use it as a springboard to get elected to public office as soon as he can. He's not an educator. He's a politician."

"He was a barber before he became Director," James went on. "If you want a cheap haircut just ask Soto for one. He'll know how to clip you."

"The guy is doing me a favor. I don't care what he was. I'll be able to make some money and start pulling my own weight around here. You wouldn't mind that, would you?"

"It's about time," was all James said. Then, "We're running low on weed. You said you met some guys we could get from? I'm not about to go over to Roy Johnsons' pig pen if I can help it."

"Yeah. I met them hitchhiking. Gay guys."

"Gays?"

"Yeah. When I get back from Salinas tomorrow we can try and score some weed from them. Then we'll celebrate my new job."

"How about some women to celebrate with, James? Don't you know any?"

I'd been without Lena too long. I'd been without a woman too long. I was horny as hell. My balls were aching. I needed and wanted sex. Love didn't matter.

"What about your girlfriend, Mr. Clean?"

"I want to get laid."

"I'm sworn off sex," James said with such a serious face I thought he was putting me on.

"Sworn off?" I said, taking the bait. "How can you swear off something you have to do?"

"Who says you have to do it?"

"You didn't swear off eating, did you?"

"Eating? Jesus. What's eating got to do with sex?"

"I just thought they might be the same."

"You should mind your own damn business," James blurted out, rubbing his jaw like a philosopher.

"Don't the kids you advise at school ask you about sex?" I continued to badger him.

"Sure they do. Every day."

"What do you tell them?"

"Don't be ashamed of your feelings. They come from God."

"You don't practice what you preach. If you think they should do it then how come you don't?"

Seeing I had James at a standstill I continued to harass him, "You're one of the smartest guys I know. You give the best advice there is on almost every subject. I know you speak from experience most of the time too. But when it comes to sex you're out of your fucking mind."

"Fuck you, too!" he vehemently interrupted me.

He continued, "I've had my share of problems with women just like every guy I know. And damn, it's hard laying off. It's a lot easier for me doing without sex than begging for it. My self respect is more important to me than a piece of ass. I've had plenty of pain from women. Maybe too much. I tried hard to form relationships. I discovered I wasn't a glutton for that type of punishment."

He started to light another joint and I said, "Take it easy with that stuff in case we can't get from those guys tomorrow." James didn't hear a word I said as he continued smoking and talking, "I used to keep myself in top fucking form. I wanted to attract women. After the struggles I went through for a piddling orgasm I discovered that no price was worth it.

THERES NO VACATION FROM DESIRE

After you've been pussy whipped you either do without, do too much, or turn into a cunt yourself. All them faggots hate women. They hate half the human race. That's because they're so prone to being pussy whipped they avoid and ridicule their greatest fear."

He usually had me in arguments when he was cold and calculating and could think fast, but when the issue was hot I had him cold and got the best of him, "There's another thing I've wanted to ask you for a long time now, James."

"What's that?" he answered, still defensive, though trying not to show it. "You counsel those nutty kids out there in the Quonset hut, and you say you can recognize what's wrong with them because you've been through it."

"That's right."

"What the hell do you tell them? Use drugs and not fuck. Is that the answer?"

"You don't have to be cured to know what the cure is. I don't know what the ultimate remedy is. I emphasize coping. The ones who hang in there the best make it."

"Man is not a perfect creature," James lectured. "His anatomy and mind have built in mistakes. All anyone can do is acknowledge our imperfections because there just aren't any panaceas for our state of evolution. Man is an incomplete work. Life is dealing with our defects as well as we can. Some aren't born equipped to stand up to the conditions of human existence. They get sick. Mentally and physically. They feel like they were never meant for this world."

"All I can conclude after almost dying is that life is a mystery and impossible to understand. The best thing you can do is learn how to take it well. You probably won't find that in any textbooks either. But I know. It happened to me and I know what's best. If that doesn't answer your God damned nosy questions then nothing will. Now get out of my face."

The next morning Mr. Soto met me at his office door and vigorously shook my hand, congratulating me, saying, "I received word from our main office in San Jose and they approved your credentials. You have to take a little drive up there so they can complete your paper work. Welcome aboard."

He seemed happy. I was relieved. His style of doing business seemed sincere and personal. Soon I found that was just a ruse employed by an unscrupulous pretender. But when a man that seems kind is offering me a job that would finally get me settled, it put me in a great mood. There was only one problem.

"Mr. Franklin," Mr. Soto said. "In case you haven't heard. My organization has a big conflict with the Adult School in this town. The position you're about to fill here has supplied teachers for them for the past year or so. It's a matter of salary and benefits you understand. They seem to think stealing my personnel is a joke of some kind. In lieu of that I must ask you to promise to work here for at least one year."

Although I knew he didn't have a legal right to make that request, and it burned me to have to agree to be an indentured servant, and almost told him to shove the job, I said, "Sure. I'm just glad you're giving me the opportunity to make a living."

Directly after our discussion the boss began motoring me around. Salinas is a big small town. Our first stop was at the political meeting house of his party, a Democratic-Mexican coalition group. An American

THERES NO VACATION FROM DESIRE 81

flag was hanging on a white pole in front of the building. Mr. Soto said, "This is a unscheduled stop. I'll only be a few minutes."

On the way to our unscheduled stop he had informed me that the Jobs Congress relies on federal funds, and that he has to constantly take into account and cater to all the people that can help keep his school supplied with students and money. When I once or twice asked him something about the curriculum he seemed not even to know what the word meant.

He kept me waiting in the car for a long time. Perhaps a half hour. He arrived in a huff, and said, "Sorry. I was on the phone talking to my man in Washington. I may have to fly out there next week."

"Sounds important," I said.

He laughed.

We drove to an outlying industrial district of Salinas where the Jobs Congress owned and used a warehouse as part of their school. I wouldn't be working in this building, but Mr. Soto wanted to show me how extensive their operation was. I was impressed. The staff seemed competent and friendly there too. Just like the instructors at the downtown site, they weren't state certified, but were people who had spent years at their jobs, and knew what they were doing. Rather than earning college credits they earned a living, and that now qualified them to teach there. My college degree was unusual among the Jobs Congress staff as far as I could tell. With jobs so difficult to find I don't know why that should be?

In the gray cinder block warehouse, big enough to be used as an airplane hangar, was the car mechanic and welding programs. All the enormous machines seemed to be new and modern. I was sure this was the most expensive part of their program, although it wasn't the most visible.

I also remember being struck by the vapidness of the young students. They wouldn't do anything on their own. Perhaps they were intimidated by the cost of the machinery? Perhaps it was one of the safety regulations there? It didn't seem like the pupils were learning how to think.

The one teacher I observed closely knew his stuff. He had worked around machinery like this for such a long time that it didn't bother him in the least what problems would come up. He'd seen it all. Everything was just a variation of something else, either good or problematic.

While drinking a cup of coffee drawn form a stainless steel industrial sized urn in a glass walled office adjacent to the working floor of the auto mechanics section, a scraping sound so loud, and a scorching scent so powerful, filled the little unventilated room so quickly, that everyone reacted with motion instead of words.

What we saw was a tractor and plow slowly crossing the cement floor. There was no driver, and the jammed action of the plow was causing sparks so big and bright it seemed to be lightning coming from the depths of the earth instead of the skies.

"Damn stupid bastards," Juan Soto said to no one in particular, calculating how much damage would be done by the slow moving vehicle and plow trying to furrow a solid cement floor. It looked like someone was going to be electrocuted or crushed.

Work experienced instructors were trying to mount the machine before it burrowed into a wall or some other machinery. The man trying to jump on was quiet with determination, but a group of gawking students were pointing the finger at a small guilty looking boy with a simple lettuce field face.

The tractor had a mind of its own and changed direction heading for the glass walled office we had been drinking coffee in. The lady secretary who stayed in the office bailed out of what she thought was a safe place screaming and hollering for help.

The out of control conveyance crashed through the combination wall-window, smashing it, ruining the office and itself. The vehicle then burst into flames. We had evacuated outside except for a few brave souls who fought the fire with extinguishers. The fire department arrived quickly and within minutes put the inferno out. Everything returned to a state of post disaster tranquilized serenity.

"You'd better try and make it home from here on your own," Juan Soto told me, very calm and remote. "I'll be here for a long time. Don't forget your appointment in San Jose tomorrow morning." He entered the smoldering smoking warehouse with a look of disappointment so strong I thought it might kill him.

Chapter 7

"Do you know the way to San José?" Oh yeah. I just don' have anything to get there with. So James loaned me his truck while he went about his business on his "Lone Wolf" motorcycle, which by the way, he'd built himself. The bike was as big and as fast as any honcho Hells Angels.

Ralph was already sitting out on the back sundeck as I was leaving for San Jose early that morning. He was basking in the eastern sun, and was sipping coffee from a silver red striped thermos. As soon as the day turns hot he gets the cooler filled with beer out there.

"Where's to today?" Ralph asked me. "Jimmy told me you may be sticking around?"

"I am."

"I'm glad to hear it. That boy's been a lot happier since you got here. Someone to listen to his music I guess."

Ralph just arrived back from driving his Japanese girlfriend to work. She didn't speak English so we'd never spoken, but she had a beautiful smile that conveyed a friendliness that words couldn't. I don't know how long she's been living in this country?

James stuck his short haired head out our door, grimacing from the sun in his eyes, and said to me. "There's a full tank in her now. And that's the way I want her back. Morning Ralph. Got a half a cup for me? I'm waiting for my water to boil."

"They'll be a tank and a half in her when I bring her back", I said to James, descending the broad wooden steps, adjusting the knot in my tie. Waiting around for jobs I'd lost the habit of wearing good duds and wasn't comfortable in dress clothes anymore. It didn't seem right to be formal in this climate anyway.

We'd scored the weed from the gay guys, Ron and Clark. It was very good home grown. I had a few doobies rolled and ready to smoke on my way back to Monterey later in the day after I'd taken care of business. I had called ahead and told Clark I was in need of some weed. He told me if I came over then he'd be able to help me out. I didn't tell him I was bringing James with me.

The couple were gardening in the front yard of their New Monterey cottage. The lush flora was multicolored with a variety of specimens whose pleasing scents filled the air. The belt high newly painted white picket fence enclosing the small yard appeared charmingly rickety and antique. The house was tiny. A doll house. "There they are, James. Out front there. See them?"

"Yeah. Maybe we won't even have to go in."

"Maybe."

James stopped the truck in front of the cottage next to a sidewalk that was cracked and broken from time and use.

"Hi," I said through the truck window to the gardeners at work on their own plot.

"Hiya too," Clark returned with a flourish of his hands, returning my greeting. Ron was very curious as to who was doing the driving and stared rudely at James as he got out from behind the wheel. My cousin and I entered the gate at the side into the dense garden. We shook hands all

THERES NO VACATION FROM DESIRE 87

around. Ron went inside while Clark stayed out front and spoke with us.

"If we don't pull the weeds up once a week we get swamped with them," Clark said. "The work is worth it though. Getting to live in such a beautiful house."

"Yeah. Nice little place you've got here," James said kindly, letting no barriers come between us and a score.

"We've got plenty of what you need," Clark bubbled with his delicate diction.

"Come on inside," he invited us. As we followed him up the three red steps into the house we noticed the buns of his ass were hanging out from the bottoms of his very short cutoff jeans. James wasn't wearing his headgear and was dumfoundedly looking at the inverts butt.

"The fags in San Francisco are exhibitionists too," James whispered in my ear. Clark turned around, used to having people talk behind his back. "Did you say something?" he challenged James with his tone. "I'm sorry. I didn't hear what you said?"

"I was just admiring your buttercups on the window sill", James replied. "We sent all the way to a hot house in Kansas City for them. Our house is loaded with seeds. We have so many we have no place to plant them."

I was surprised by the dank gloominess of the interior of the cottage. It was in such startling contrast to the outside of the place. It reminded me of a beautiful woman with no internal qualities. Comely and elegant on the surface. Dark and degraded in the spirit.

The lights were so dim inside that it seemed we entered a movie house. My eyes had to get used to the light before I could find my seat. James was rubbing his eyes too, bringing them around to a level where he could see. Through the darkness I could observe a low wattage naked bulb in a ceiling socket, but its glow was hardly illuminating anything.

"Ron is putting together an ounce for you," Clark said, my eyes getting used to the shadowy atmosphere, the room seeming to get brighter all by itself. When I looked at James he was on his knees in front of a huge fish tank that had an awesome amount of sea life in it. When Clark turned on the tanks interior, hidden lights, the fish seemed to have put on their best suit of scales to please viewers. James, finding something to interest him without having to delve into the overt, incense laden sexuality of the hut, said to Clark, "Amusing collection of fish. I've always wanted to do this for myself". "It's not difficult. But you always have to take care of them. They die on us all the time. Especially the exotic expensive ones we go to San Francisco to buy."

We approached the threshold to the kitchen which was immediately behind the small living room we were leaving. Ron emerged from the bathroom, naked as a tuna, wiping his cock with a towel, and talking to us at the same time, as though this were normal behavior. He said, "I'll get that ounce for you right away. I just wanted to freshen up a little first. I get so hot and sweaty working in the yard. I'll be right back". Then he disappeared.

"I'll be with you in a moment," Clark said, directing us into the kitchen, telling us to take a seat, and angry look on his feminine face as he went in the same direction as his flashy lover.

There were so many wall and ceiling plants in the kitchen we had to karate chop our way through the torrid jungle to an opening where the kitchen table was and where we could sit down unmolested by branches.

"Pretty weird shit," James said to me in a level only I could hear.

"You're not kidding," I said.

"In the locker room you don't think anything of it. But with these guys in here. Jesus. These guys are sick, Jack. They don't even know us and they're stripping like whores. Weird shit."

"Let's just get the stuff and get out of here as fast as we can."

"Good plan."

The odd couple entered the tropical hot house kitchen and Ron asked, "Do you want a lemonade or something?"

"No thanks," James said. I didn't answer. A marijuana plant looked to be the dominant shrub in the room. It took up an entire corner. It must've taken them a long time to grow it.

"We've been getting high off that plant for a year now," Clark said proudly. "That's where this stuff comes from," he continued, rolling the plastic bagged ounce of weed onto the table. James picked it up and stuck his nose into the bag. After taking a deep breath he concluded, "It smells like the real thing."

"It is," Clark promised, as James paid him.

"You want to smoke with us?" Ron lisped.

"No thanks," I said, probably insulting them.

Driving the highway north to San Jose I had the feeling I was at the beginning of something that was going to settle me in life. It was only a job though. A low paying one too. But driving through the cool morning air among the brown coastal mountains, traffic so light it seemed like I had the whole road to myself, I experienced a revelation that I am doing the right thing with my life, taking my chances this way. Everything that gives you momentum comes from unplanned and unintended chance. I felt I'd be able to tell Lena to come on out so we could live together. Everything looked rosy.

Not far into my drive I spotted a hitchhiker with a sign in her hand that spelled out SAN FRANCISCO. The closer I got the closer her details got. She was wearing a pink tie-dyed t-shirt with SPACE CADET printed across the front.

"I'm going to San Jose. Need a ride?"

Her name was Gail. She was as beautiful as a woman could look. She fit all my dreams of a California golden girl. She was talkative and inquisitive from the moment she entered the truck, and conversation was nonstop. I was thinking if she lived in Monterey County I'd try and find out where.

"Oh no. I'm from LA. I've got friends in San Francisco I'm on my way to see."

"You've just come from LA?"

"No. I've been at the Watkins Clinic in Big Sur for a month. That's where all my money went. I feel wonderful now though. They sure know what's ailing the human race," she said, as though she were an expert on that subject.

I thought she may be a nut when she mentioned she just came from a clinic. I questioned her some more about it, never hearing about Watkins before. "It's a sex clinic. It's world famous. I'm surprised you never heard of it living around here."

"I just moved here a couple of months ago."

She talked about sex as easily as Ron displayed it in his cottage in Monterey. She wasn't ashamed and spoke in a combination of her own language combined with newly learned clinical expressions. I discussed sex with her just as easily as I'd talk with Ralph about the Korean war.

"I had lots of problems before I went to Watkins. I just wasn't into it."
"Not into what?"
"Making love."
"Oh," I said. "Now you like to do it?"
"Yes," she brightened, "more than anything else in the world. But they had to teach me to like it." I thought I'd better keep this conversation on and informative level, because, although she was a svelte blonde beauty, she couldn't have been more than eighteen, and she seemed so mixed up and trusting it would've disturbed me to violate that confidence.

"Why did they have to teach you to like something you were born to like? I know a guy just like you. He stays away from sex."
"I was conditioned by others not to like it. The problem is that a lot of people think it's a sin to make love. They bring religion into it. My father is very religious. He forbid me from seeing boys."
"Aren't most parents like that though? They want to protect their children."
"They want to protect us from something they don't understand. They want to protect us from something that we want to do and should do and were created to do. God gave us sex. It's fun. It's healthy."
"You know, you're safe talking to me this way, but if you said stuff like this to the wrong guy he'd take you up on it so fast you might lose your taste for it again."

"Never," giggled the space cadet. "You're so attractive I'd love to make it with you. Why don't we stop somewhere?"

I felt sorry for her being so vulnerable to her pleasure instinct. I wondered if the Watkins Clinic had done the right thing for her. I wanted to help her, to tell her my beliefs, to acknowledge to her that all she's feeling and doing is fine if done in the right place at the right time. She smile innocently and sweetly at me thinking she possessed the true answer to living the ideal life.

When everything seemed to be perfect again I heard that loud threatening buzzing roar coming from behind me on the highway. I knew what was coming.

I glanced through the rearview mirror to see how close they were, but couldn't see them at all. The din of their combined motors was very loud. Since I hadn't been seen by The Losers yet I thought I might turn off the main road onto a subsidiary route until they passed.

If they recognized James' truck I wouldn't have a chance without James to help me. The space cadet was napping with her head on my lap, trusting strangers dangerously. Within moments, through the mirror, I saw so many motorcycles coming up from behind me it looked like a locust disaster. Going over a rising ridge in the road I could see where the swarm started, but couldn't spot the end. I was looking back so much I almost ran a cow over that was standing on the side of the highway. The cadet slept soundly, snoring slightly, drooling on my pants.

The gang was riding in a quadruple column formation across the entire highway. They were one vehicle. The bikers wore their colors, their sleeveless denim jackets. An assortment of helmets appeared, including a horned Viking war bonnet. I drove slowly expecting the worst.

The squad of bikes began passing me and not bothering me. As the first few went past I looked at their colors and saw that these were the Hells Angels. The sun reflected brightly off a group within the group, wearing chrome helmets and riding together.

The first hundred or so that went by had their colors captioned with OAKLAND, and then they started appearing with LOS ANGELES on their backs. Other than an occasional glance at me they were minding their own business. In fact, more than just a few of them, when they saw me gaping at them, laughed, and saluted me as though in the military. I was flattered being greeted by The Angels that way.

It took them at least twenty minutes to pass me on their way to wherever it was they were going. It appeared to be a council of some type. A meeting of the north and south tribes. I wasn't about to bother them to learn their business. I had my own to take care of.

When we arrived in San Jose Gail woke up. She was groggy with sleep and it was evident she was still exhausted. No telling how hard they worked her at the clinic the past few weeks.

"You'll have to get the rest of the way another way," I said. "Do you have any money in case you get stuck?"

"No. That's why I'm going to San Francisco. To get some money," she said, yawning and stretching.

In downtown gritty palm treed San Jose I espied the bus terminal and knew I wanted to do her a favor. I let her off and gave her five dollars for a ticket so she could get to her destination without having to feel obligated to perform sex acts as a medium of exchange. She never bothered asking me where I lived in Monterey. I didn't try finding out where she was going.

"Thank you mister", she said when I gave her the money.
"I love you", she smiled.
"I love you too," I said.

Not far from the bus depot, on a street shady with palm trees, was the sprawling building I was looking for. The address on the plate glass door matched the one I was seeking. As you enter you find yourself standing in a huge fluorescent lighted lobby where hundreds of people are loitering, waiting for the next class to begin.

Almost all of them were racial minority people. Of all the minorities there the majority were Mexicans. Blacks were prevalent too, a group that seemed to have no presence at the Salinas branch.

Most of the students looked serious, cheerful too, to be getting some education. There looked to be a sprinkling of delinquent types, stipend collectors, enrolled there too. They used the educational system as welfare. But you knew that the Jobs Congress was making money off each one of them too. When I asked directions from a few students they couldn't understand me, nor me them. Because of a language barrier.

I eventually found a secretary behind a white wooden desk, and

THERES NO VACATION FROM DESIRE

when I told her who I was and what my business was, she said, "We've been expecting you, Mr. Franklin. Won't you have a seat. Mr. Freeze will be right out to see you." She directed me to a row of classroom seats and desks that were now used as lobby chairs.

They only kept me waiting five minutes. A young man with a trimmed beard wearing a suit that was well pressed and tailored to his physique asked me if I was Jack Franklin. When I told him I was he shook my hand and asked me to follow him to a private room that was a short distance up a freshly painted industrial corridor.

Before he asked me anything, he congratulated me on being hired by Mr. Soto. "The hiring process was completed in Salinas. This is not an interview. We just wanted to get the payroll records accurate so you can receive your proper wages. You can start working in Salinas tomorrow."

He was still interested in reading my resume. As I filled out the financial forms he gave me, he said, "It's rare for us to have certified teachers on our staff. You're the exception here." I wasn't particularly flattered by that statement since it didn't mean any more money for me.

Chapter 8

I arrived from San José to an empty apartment from my greatest California triumph yet. No one was inside or out. I couldn't hear anything but fog horns and sea lion grunts coming from the bay. Such a great day, I thought, and no one to share it with.

I dialed Lenas' New York number just to surprise her at an odd time. It was an unscheduled call at an unscheduled time. The reason was good. So what, how much it would cost. I was working now and it didn't matter in the least.

"I have the news you've been waiting for. Pack your bags and come on out. I'm all set."

"I think you have the wrong number, mister," was the reply from a woman I'd never heard before. I read the digits back to her to confirm my mistake, but she told me I had the right number and that she was Lenas' new roommate.

"She's still in bed," the girl said, groggy like, as though she'd just got out of bed.

"Tell her I'm calling", I said.

While waiting for Lena to come to the phone I could her a cat meowing. New roommate? New cat?

"Hello Love," Lena said in a voice so soothing and pleasing to me that I was immediately relaxed.

Before I began questioning her about her new friend, I said, "I just landed a job. I'll be making all the money we need. Why don't you start making plans now. I can send you some cash in a week or two."

She characteristically took her time replying, saying with her sexy bass telephone voice, "Sweetie, I don't think I want to go to California anymore." Shivers of fear and disappointment started running along my spinal nerves. She sang a few lines from the White Album, "Honey Pie, you are making me crazy. I'm in love but I'm lazy, so won't you please come home." Then she laughed a little.

"What's that?" I asked when I heard background noise again.

"Just a little puss," she said. "She's sitting on my lap now. She belongs to my new roommate, Maryanne. Maryanne moved in last week. We know each other from the dance studio. Here," Lena said, putting the damn cat on the line. "Listen to her purr when I rub her."

"The problem Lena is that I want you to come here. As soon as you can. There's no point wasting any more time. I want you to pack. Make your plans. Tell me how much money you need. I'll send it to you."

"But I don't want to go to California. Not now. I don't want to go to California", she said again, so brutally that I knew her mind was made up to go in a new direction. I could feel her leaving me out of her life. "Why did you call at such a strange time of day. You caught me at a bad time. I didn't want to talk with you this way, but you caught me at a bad time. We may as well talk about it."

"What?" I said, knowing already, and not able to sound like I wasn't pleading with her. "Go ahead and talk. I don't have anything else to do right now."

"You know I love you baby, but we've been apart for a long time. I've changed."

When I couldn't say anything, she said, "You left me without any regard for my feelings. You told me you were going and you were gone within a week. Do you know what you put me through? Do you know that I almost died when you left me? It made me stop and think. It made

THERES NO VACATION FROM DESIRE

me think you didn't love ME anymore. I honestly feel you don't know if you do love me or not. Why did you go ? I would've married you in a second. You changed so fast I still can't believe it. You frightened me. I lost my confidence. How do I know what you'll do next? Sometimes I think you cleared out just to hurt me. I really do. What else can I think why you left so fast with your shitty promises of California. I never wanted to go out there in the first place. I've met some new people since you left."

Hardening myself to the grim reality of the crisis, I said, "All right. Don't cry. You're right. Everything you said is right. I couldn't admit these things to myself before. I love you for telling the truth."

Since she had been repressing her genuine feelings in her letters, the truth gushed out the first chance it had. I was sinking. She was the reason I ran. She was always on my mind. What could my incentive be to continue to be? What are the things worth having in life?

When the mind blitzing life changing conversation ended I smoked a couple of joints rolled in double papers to make them burn slower to prevent myself from ODing. The apartment was as hot as an extermination camp killing oven. The sun outside was feverishly intense in the late afternoon.

I grabbed James' greasy black substance in the flat tin can. Looking in the mirror I made long lines of black under each of my eyes. I picked up the basketball and spun it on my finger like a Globe Trotter, for an indefinite amount of time.

I took James' headgear from the rack in the kitchen, and when I placed it on my head the visor covered my entire face. I gazed out at the world through a darkened tint. This getup didn't look so bad once you realized it was personal style and shouldn't be tampered with. I made a mental note not to hassle James the next time he wore these things.

Dribbling the ball across the rear wooden sundeck on my way to the yard, Ralph was just arriving, pulling his car into the driveway. When he saw me coming down the steps while he was still at the bottom, he said, "Jimmy boy. School's out?"

"I'm Jack," I said as though I didn't want to.

"What is this? Halloween," Ralph guffawed. "You playing a joke on your old sergeant?" he continued to laugh.

"This is no joke," I said to him, as we passed each other in opposite directions near the bottom of the steps.

Ralph seemed to be physically deteriorating at a faster pace than he thought he would. He could hardly make it up the steps without doing a combination hop, skip, duck walk, along with an incessant head bob.

"What's doing?" the kindly Medal of Honor winner asked when he was high and I was low on the steps.

"Shooting hoops."

"I used to do that too," was his concluding remark as he spasmatically ascended the steps at a snails pace.

I took twenty quick foul shots sinking eighteen of them. I started playing against an imaginary opponent who was twice my size and of greater ability. I twisted and turned and drove on him with my best moves to get my points. I couldn't be stopped. After sinking one, I turned, and

THERES NO VACATION FROM DESIRE

to my surprise saw James playing defense between me and the hoop. His grim expression told me he was all business.

"You better get out of my way or I'll put you in the hole too," I warned him.

"Anytime you're ready," was his challenging reply. I drove down the lane. He stuck his hand out hacking my arm, and I called a foul on him. He grinned till he laughed, and said, "This is my court. Anything goes. No fouls allowed."

I wanted to school him about playing fair, but I realized we were inventing a game of our own, and that was more fun than playing by the rules. I drove on him again with no intention of avoiding contact. I leaped up and towards the basket. We collided in air. The ball went in the hoop. We lost our balance and slammed onto the cement pavement of the driveway. We got up laughing.

"Good shot!" was all James said, as though we were playing by an approved set of rules.

After a few more minutes of brawling shoving contact we settled into a legitimate game, and I discovered that James had some decent skills on the basketball court too. The guy could do anything. Too bad he was crazy. He never even questioned me about wearing his face covering headgear. I guess he didn't have to ask. He already knew why people protected themselves like that.

I was relieved from my afternoon phone call with Lena. All the exercise and contact eased me. In our apartment I was able to remove James' headgear and wash the black lines off my face. I didn't need them anymore.

"Are you set with the Jobs Congress now?" James asked.

"Yeah. I'm in. I start tomorrow."

"That's great," he said. "I was suspended from my teaching job today. You'll have to carry us for awhile."

"What does that mean?" I asked, astonished.

"It means," he said, slowly and intelligently, "that I don't go to work in the morning and I don't make any money."

"Tell me what happened?" I asked, amused. "I've got to hear this. You must've really pulled something this time."

"No. It wasn't much," he said, so nonchalantly he seemed to be sitting on top of the world. "Besides, I think I have something else lined up already. Got a joint rolled?"

"Yeah. Over there on the table."

When he saw how much was left from this morning he said, "What the hell you been doing with this stuff, making brownies?"

"No, just smoking it. I had some bad news this afternoon when I got back from San Jose. Tell me what happened to you first."

"You know how it is between the Mexican and white kids in Salinas?"

"Yeah," I said.

"Just like all the experts, I have my own ideas on how things should be worked out. I have systems I believe in. They work. They're not in the textbooks, but they work." My heavy afternoon gloom was lightened some more by James' story, and the flippant, cavalier way he was telling it.

"When I'm working with those kids out in the Quanset huts," James continued, "whenever something racial happened between a couple of them, if they couldn't talk the issue out, I'd take them out in back of the hut and make them swing out in a fist fight."

"Holy shit!" I didn't know what to think. "Isn't that extreme?"

"Isn't the problem extreme?" he said, bored to have to point out something so obvious to me.

"Whenever I made a couple of kids fight it out they always ended up with a great deal of respect for each other. No matter what the outcome was. They didn't see each other as stereotypes anymore. You can't beat up or get beaten up by a stereotype. Only people can do that to each other."

"Word of what I was doing got back to the principal, Sender. He told me he had to suspend me without pay because my methods were so unorthodox and scandalous. The parents were calling for my head. Now I'm out. I doubt if I'll be going back there."

The next morning, my first paid day of work in months, I caught a ride to Salinas with James. He dropped me off on Main Street, before going to meet with Mr. Sender. Entering the clean white washed Jobs Congress building as a full fledged faculty member, nothing worried or bothered me. I was on the offensive.

Upon entering Mr. Sotos' office I perceived a room full of businessmen discussing financial matters not only for education, but for other pet programs the group cherished too.

"Ah, Mr. Franklin. Good morning," Mr. Soto greeted me in front of the congregation. "Are you ready for your ride? You must be getting tired of all this traveling? Two days in a row to San Jose. We usually schedule our agenda much better than this. I apologize and promise you things will run a lot smother from now on."

Turning our attention to the five man panel sitting around a dark wood conference table, Mr. Soto introduced me to them, saying, "Gentlemen. Mr. Franklin is the newest member of our faculty here. He's so new he hasn't even started yet", he added, making an attempt at humor. Then he introduced each man to me.

"Mr. Torres. Our accountant. Mr. Mendez. President of our political party in Salinas. Mr. Crespo. Our man in Washington. He came to California to listen to our problems for a little while. And Joe Rivera. A citizen. A friend. A believer in the Jobs Congress. Mr. Perez. Our banker. Mr. Franklin," Mr. Soto went on "will be teaching our general education class here. He's going to San Jose today to observe our program there. Bill Henry teaches general ed up there. He's been doing it since we started. We thought Mr. Franklin could get some ideas from watching the master at work."

Turning to me Mr. Soto asked, "Do you think you'll get enough guidance watching Bill Henry to run your own program?"

"I'm sure it will help. I'm sure it will get me off to a good start."

"By the way, gentleman," Mr. Soto persisted, standing at the head of the table, his right index finger raised like a college professor making a point, "Mr. Franklin is the first teacher on our staff with a college degree." I immediately, and for the first time felt victimized by Mr. Sotos' remarks. Not only was I a vastly underpaid teacher, but a certified token for Mr. Soto to show off, perhaps useful for accumulating more funds for the program. I smiled at the room full of strangers.

When I was dismissed from the meeting I was still in need of a ride to San Jose. The Jobs Congress couldn't or wouldn't arrange transportation for their college boy. It was already two strikes on Mr. Soto as far as I was concerned. The company that hired me wouldn't help me. I was trying to solve my problem alone.

Entering the front lobby I noticed a man standing at the Coke machine. It sure looked like he was wearing the suit that was stolen from me by The Losers. I held back from approaching him thinking I might have trouble on my hands if I involved myself with a Loser. His back was turned to me. He didn't look like the same person I exchanged clothing with because his hair was short now. I remembered his tree trunk forearms though, and didn't want to mess around with him if I didn't have to.

"Mr. Jones," the Spanish secretary called my suit from her position behind her desk. "All your papers have been processed. You were lucky. You were the last entry for this quarter. It would've been a long wait if you hadn't come in when you did."

Still with his back to me, still unsure if it was the Loser, I heard him say, very loud, tremorusly and preacherishly, "Jesus brought me back to the flock on time. He showed me the way. He brought me here after he showed me the right path." When I heard his voice I knew he was the filthy slob I exchanged clothing with out at Roy Johnsons' pig pen palace in Seaside.

The secretary glanced at the Loser with an amused smile, and said, "They're waiting for you at the machine shop now, Mr. Jones. Your stipend money will start when you punch the time clock over there. You're prepared to start today I hope?"

"Yes maam," was the Losers humble reply, showing her his little brown sack containing his lunch. "All set, maam."

"Very good. Just wait a moment. I have to ask Mr. Soto something about your application. Nothing to worry about. Just a technicality."

"Sure maam. I understand."

Although we were the only people in the lobby he was too shy to look at me. I took the liberty to study him as much as I could. "Ah, Mr. Jones," I said, approaching him, catching him by surprise. Upon hearing his name he flinched slightly, and for a moment I thought he was going to put his hands defensively over his head.

"Yes sir?" he asked, having no idea of who I was.

"I'm Mr. Franklin. I work here."

"I'm Clyde Jones," he said, putting a glad hand out for me to shake. "I start working on car motors today. Over at the machine shop."

"Don't you know me?" I asked him.

"No. I don't," he said with apprehension in his voice, seriously sizing me up. "Do I know you?"

"Should I?"

"I wouldn't have recognized you either if I hadn't noticed you wearing a suit that was stolen from me."

His lack of sophistication and his frequent fortune of being caught in the wrong came into play.

"Yes yes. Now I know you. And I owe you a great deal, mister. Yes. This IS your suit. I'm not ashamed to say. Getting a hold of your clothes was a blessing for me, Mr. Franklin." He was about nineteen, but appeared much younger now with short hair and a clean shaven face. He was childlike and immature.

"I don't want to cause you any trouble Clyde, but don't you think I should be paid for my suit?"

"Yes sir. I sure do. No doubt about that", he said, apparently really having changed his ways.

"If you give me the opportunity I'll gladly pay you back. Just as soon as I can. In a few weeks. I'm clean now. I quit The Losers. I want to pay you back. I wish there was something I could do before my paycheck comes. I know. Why don't you come to the church meeting tomorrow night? I'll be able to treat you right there."

"No. That's okay," I said, seeing that this man was making a hearty effort to improve and to live in harmony with himself.

"And don't worry about paying me back," I said. "I'm just glad that things are starting to work out for you."

"Excuse me sir," he said , as though insulted. "But I owe you something and I won't feel right until I can even it up."

"Forget it," I said, as the secretary reentered the lobby saying to Clyde, "Just go over to the machine shop now and everything will work out fine." In the same breath she said to me, "Have you got transportation yet to San Jose, Mr. Franklin?"

"No. I guess I'm taking the bus."

"Use my car," the saved one said. I thought this resolution would give Clyde the feeling of atonement he craved, plus it would be much easier for me to get to San Jose.

"Will you be at the Jobs Congress all day?" I asked Clyde.

"Yup. Until four thirty. You can take my car and be back by then, right?"

"Yes. If you don't mind me driving your car", I replied, not wanting to force him into anything.

"I don't mind, mister. I want to do it. Take my car and bring it back this afternoon to the machine shop. I'll still be there."

"Well, if you think it's alright I will."

"Jesus told me it's all right."

The first thing I noticed about Clydes' car, other than it being in good shape and looked like it ran well, were the bumper stickers on the rear. The first one was red with a white cross in each corner of it, with the words HONK THREE TIMES IF YOU LOVE JESUS. Next to the directional, on the extreme right side of the bumper was a white sticker with red words that read I"D RATHER BE PRAYING. Finally, the biggest sticker, on the left side of the bumper read JESUS IS JUST ALRIGHT WITH ME. My first thought though was to try and get out of using this car because it looked queer.

The top of the dashboard had so many magnetized God-fearing statues and emblems on it that it felt like we were in a mobile church on our way to baptize the world. "Don't these things distract you?" I asked Clyde, as we made our way to the machine shop.

"No. I can drive under any conditions," he said, for the first time hinting at his very recent former life. I wanted to ask him about the motorcycle gang, more from curiosity than anything else, but since we were rapidly approaching our destination I decided not to.

While walking to the driver's side of the car, passing around in front of it, I noticed his front bumper was as congested with religious messages as his rear one. He left the motor running, and by the time he could say "Amen" I was on my way north.

The roads were clear and straight. Not an obstacle in the way.

THERES NO VACATION FROM DESIRE

Almost half way through my ride, near Gilroy, a tan van came up next to me on my left. Every few seconds the driver beeped his horn three times. I thought he was signaling me to check out a low tire or something. When I looked at those within the van I saw a group of nuns waving and smiling benevolently at me. I remembered the bumper sticker telling all those who love Jesus to honk three times. I smiled and waved back. Although I was traveling in Gods' own limousine, that was the only religious experience I had that day. Most people ignored me, probably thinking I was some type of odd crank.

Just like in Salinas, the Jobs Congress in San Jose had two separate buildings in different parts of town. I parked in front of the branch I hadn't been to yet. It looked like a factory from the outside.

I was expected by the staff there. As soon as they knew I was there I was led to a classroom on the first floor. I was there to observe a master teacher that had been running this class successfully for ten years. He had helped many people get jobs. Since I still didn't have a clear idea of what I was actually supposed to teach, and how I was supposed to go about it, it helped me immensely to talk with this man and to observe him.

The classroom was filled to capacity with perhaps fifty students. They were all young men and women, and almost all of them were minority folk. The atmosphere in the room was pleasant. It seemed like most of the students enjoyed being where they were.

There wasn't an empty wall in the room. Every square inch, from the middle of the wall to the ceiling, was covered with rules and regulations concerning the art of finding, interviewing, being hired, and then being good at your job.

The teacher, Bill Henry, was in his late forties. He was shaggy haired, wrinkled rough from the outdoors, and displayed a tattoo on his lower left bicep, just under his white shirt sleeve that was rolled up a ways. A pack of cigarettes was in his shirt pocket. He spoke well and softly, and with respect, to every student. It seemed like he had a lot of street smarts to go along with his low key classroom demeanor.

On the front wall of the room were the numerous rules. The entire space was covered with posters, with intelligence on them, such as WEAR A SUIT, SPEAK COURTEOUSLY, BE ON TIME and DON'T SCRATCH. So many decrees that it would've been impossible to remember them all. I surmised the instructor wanted this code of the business world to be implanted in his students minds through constant exposure to them. Not memorization. Osmosis.

Mr. Henry acknowledged me after I was settled comfortably into a desk-seat near the rear of the room.
"Did you say your name is Mr. Franklin?" he asked me.
"Yes."
"Well, Mr. Franklin," he said affably, "this morning we'll be working on job interviews. We'll stage a few. Feel free to take notes if you like."

Mr. Henry removed his chair from behind his desk, sat in it, then asked a student sitting in the first row to put another chair next to his desk. He sent another student to the hallway so he could begin the mock interview.

THERES NO VACATION FROM DESIRE

"Come in," Mr. Henry said to the nonknock, as the sheepish twenty year old man entered, grinning demonstratively. Mr. Henry said to him "Please take a seat, Mr. Lopez."

"Thank you sir", answered the well mannered student, wearing apparel that was appropriate to actually go job hunting in.

"Now then, Mr. Lopez," said Mr. Henry, "how did you find out about this job."

"I want you to know, sir," the candidate replied, "that I'm applying for the job of welder. I don't want you to think I'm here for something else."

"Uh hu."

"I read the ad in the newspaper," he said, wiping the corner of his eye. Mr. Henry stopped, an obvious break from the formality of the interview, and said, "Don't move your hands around when you're talking with the interviewer. It will take away from your presence and make him think you're afraid. Now, back to the interview", Mr. Henry went on, then said, "Do you know what the work here entails, Mr. Lopez?"

"Yes sir. I recently finished a course in welding at the Jobs Congress."

"Very good. We hire a lot of people from there."

"I've been trained in all phases of welding. But the ad said not much experience was needed. It was a job for a beginner."

"Yes. That's right. You're very observant."

"What type of work did you do before going to the Jobs Congress?" Mr. Henry continued.

"I worked the fields. I picked fruit."

"You didn't like it?"

"No sir. Not at all. That's why I went to school and studied. I wanted to make an opportunity for myself."

There was a loud bang on the classroom door. I thought it was a part of the staged interview. Following a dour faced secretary into the room there were men wearing uniforms that seemed to be official. What a ploy, I thought.

The officers were armed with pistols in their holsters though, and as one of them approached Mr. Henry, who was rising from his seat as though he knew exactly what was going on, the other two officers blocked the doorway. The color of their uniforms was greenish-brown, murky. An odd tint and reminiscent of the uniforms worn by the New York City meter maids. Is this how they handle parking tickets in California?

The students were dead silent and attentive, apparently knowing the uniform and what it represented. After speaking quietly with Mr. Henry, the presiding officer said, flashing his badge to the class, "Immigration. It's reported that there are illegal aliens in this room and we're here to take you. I have three names. When you hear your name I want you to rise and go to my men over there." He was matter of fact and didn't seem to enjoy his task.

I realized that their uniforms were probably the same color as Rio Grande mud. The two subsidiary guards, stone faced and official, stood rigid and ready to apprehend the aliens.

"The names," the commanding officer said, peering at a slip of paper he held in his right hand. "Martinez, Juanita. Camacho, Dolores. Castanos, Ada."

THERES NO VACATION FROM DESIRE

Three women stood up without protest and approached the officers at the side of the room. The other students seemed to sigh with relief, and I wondered how many more of them had entered the United States illegally. Each woman was handcuffed. Both sides seemed as though they'd been through this before, and all concerned were well behaved and courteous. They left as swiftly as they entered.

Bill Henry said, "Are there any relatives to those just taken?" A woman who had been sobbing quietly broke down, and although she didn't say anything, we all knew a loved one had been taken from her. As sympathetically as possible Mr. Henry said to the well dressed woman. "You may take the rest of the day off if you wish," knowing she wanted to trail the party that just left. She went.

"Are there any questions or comments on what just happened?" the instructor asked. "If not let's try and continue as best we can."

Chapter 9

I saved enough money after a month or so on the job to buy myself an old used car. A discarded and starting to rust Mercury. I found it through an ad in the newspaper, and bought it from its owner at his house in Carmel Valley. When I first arrived there, after hitchhiking, he tried selling me a machine that wasn't listed in the paper, but which he thought I might want. But the thing smoked and burned so much oil I would've been a fool to purchase it. The car I bought needed so much minor work to get her running smoothly that I took her to the Jobs Congress auto shop. The shop was a free service for the teaching staff.

When I brought her in I asked for Clyde Jones to do the work. He knew everything about motors. When I spoke with Clyde, I said, "You get this thing working right and you won't owe me a thing. I'll owe you."

"You got it", was Clyde's reply. If I didn't have a personal mechanic working on my car at the Jobs Congress I may not have tried there at all.

I was warned by one of my faculty colleagues. Regis, a tall, balding, recently divorced, marathon bicycle riding, language teacher, being paid by the Adult School, working within the Jobs Congress, had told me, "I brought my Ford to them for a tune-up."

"It was only two years old. I was taking her on a long trip. I drove down to Los Angeles. I had no problems along the way. But the first time I was within the city limits I shut her off and she wouldn't start again. I had to get a boost to get her going and then had to get the damned thing tuned up again. The mechanic there told me the timing was so off it's a wonder she didn't explode and catch fire. That's why I never bring my car to the Jobs Congress auto shop anymore."

After telling me about the life of his car, Regis changed the subject and said, "Don't say anything to Soto. Don't tell him I'm telling you this. The Adult School is thinking about starting up their program out at the county jail again. It's not official. Bill Getz, I think you know him, was saying something about it at our last staff meeting."

"Thanks for the news," I said, "but I owe Soto some time here for hiring me."

"That prick asks everyone he hires here to work for him a year. No one stays if they get a better paying job though. Soto is an easy guy to fuck. You already know he treats everyone like shit. He doesn't deserve any loyalty."

A month after Regis told me about the county jail job I still hadn't heard anything else. I was settled comfortably into my teaching routine at the Jobs Congress. One sunny day I took one of my favorite students to lunch at a nearby Mexican fast food restaurant.

Willy was in his mid sixties, and had been at the Jobs Congress for many months past the time he should've been working. His age was difficult to place in the hiring market. He was collecting his stipend, and his wife, when healthy, worked, and they were able to afford their public housing unit at towns edge. Willy had completed his bookkeeping program and had been knocking around the general ed classes ever since. Sometimes he sat in on the grocery checking class and learned how to operate the cash registers, and how to deal with customers with coupons.

The cashier was ringing up the amount of our purchase of tamales

THERES NO VACATION FROM DESIRE

and enchiladas when the electrical power went out on the cash register. Ordinarily, after ringing up the amount of a meal, and then given an amount by the paying customer, the machine would show her, with digital lights, how much change to give back. But with the register down she didn't know how much change to make.

"I hope she's not a Jobs Congress graduate," I said to Willy.

"I've never seen her around," said the pudgy healthy looking full blooded Indian.

"They teach you how to make change at our school anyway," Willy followed up. I finally promised the young dark eyed cashier I wasn't cheating her and told her how much change I was due.

When Willy and I retired to a side table outside the building, sitting under a striped umbrella with TACO QUEEN stamped on top, he spoke a little about his life as young man. Based on his merry, mild ways, it threw me when he said, "I rode the rails for twenty years."

"You were a railroad man for all that time?"

"Some may call it that, but most called us hobos. I used to drink a lot. I almost killed myself with alcohol."

In class Willy paid such strict attention to everything, adding comments from his own experience, that he was the perfect student. He enjoyed listening to the young people too. He seemed like a frustrated genius who never had the opportunity to develop his mind, but loved the learning environment so much he could've existed for that purpose alone.

"I was born in New Mexico on a reservation. I never took a train east of the Mississippi in all the years I bummed. I was an up and down tramp. I'd go up north to Montana or Wyoming in summer, then go back south again for winter."

"Just like a bird."

From the very first morning I was teaching at the industrial school Mr. Soto was disturbing me, barging into my classroom with groups of local and sometimes national politicians and businessmen. They never stayed long enough to find out what was going on. They loitered just long enough to be a pain in the ass. The interruptions became so frequent and distracting that the students began joking about them. During these fund raising jaunts through our classroom Mr. Soto was causing the students undue stress and anxiety, at a time and place they should've felt free to make mistakes. The Director seemed like an adversary. I had to make progress in spite of him.

On the Wednesday morning before Thanksgiving the entire school was getting ready for the afternoon party. The students and staff were bringing in food and drinks, anticipating the start of the big holiday weekend. I was putting my class through a letter writing exercise. I asked them, "What would you write to a store where you bought something and then found out the product didn't work right?" I was teaching them to write a courteous letter of complaint.

As the students were silently working at their desks the door to the classroom opened for the second time that morning by Mr. Soto, bringing his second tour of supporters around to see how things got done. When he entered the room Mr. Soto said, "I hope we're not disturbing you, Mr. Franklin. It's so quiet in here like something important is going on. What are they working on?"

THERES NO VACATION FROM DESIRE

"They're writing letters of complaint." Not understanding what for, though not disturbed by the idea, Mr. Soto asked, "To whom are you going to send the letters?"

"To hypothetical destinations," I said. "I told them to think of a time when they bought something and the product didn't work right. Then I asked them to write a letter of complaint to the store. That's what they're doing now."

"Ah, a very good idea, Mr. Franklin. I never would've thought of it myself."

"I got this idea from Bill Henry in San Jose. We correspond."

"Excellent."

"Would you like to hear a couple of the letters, Mr. Soto?" He looked at his watch and said, "Yes. I think we have the time to hear one or two of them."

"Gina? I said to the pretty, smart, post secretarial trained girl, waiting for her first interview. "Are you finished with your letter yet?"

"Not yet, Mr. Franklin. Almost."

"Would you like to read what you have to the class?" I asked her, knowing the students knew I never graded them on anything, but only pointed things out to them. I had them in the habit of doing work for itself and not for grades. She was a little hesitant, but finally agreed, and Mr. Soto said, "Thank you Gina," with his warm personal smile.

Gina slowly walked to the front of the room and sat at my desk. She looked very comfortable there.

"Who is it to?" I asked her as she was about to begin. "Gliders Department Store in King City", she said, with a slight Spanish accent. The Jobs Congress ran a school bus through the Salinas Valley making stops at all the small towns there to take the students to class here. King City is the furthest away to the south. Getting closer to Salinas there's Greenfield, Soledad, Gonzales and Chular. The auto shop kept the old bus running, but many mornings it was late.

"Dear Sir. I bought a toaster at your store last Saturday. I still have the receipt. The toaster looks nice, but gets too hot on the outside. The children can't use it. They may get burned. The bread also pops out at the wrong time. Sometimes it's not done and sometimes it's done too much. It doesn't know when to pop up. Do you think I can get another toaster?"

I didn't start telling her how to make the letter more effective because of the visitors, but said, "Very good, Gina. That should get some results." Mr. Soto and the others agreed it was a good letter.

"How about another one, Mr. Soto?" I asked, thinking that as long as I had him in my room I may as well teach him how the school works even if he didn't care.

"Yes, I think we have time for one more," he replied without hesitation.

I called Hector. He blazed red through his deep brown skin, and said, "I don't think I should read mine now. It might not sound right."

"That's okay," Mr. Soto said, when an experienced teacher would have seen that Hector was in distress and should have been passed over. A few of the visiting contingent prodded Hector too, seeing how shy he was and how amusing he could be.

The brash, bright, skinny twenty year old inched forward through the classroom. His concentration was so intense that he seemed like he

THERES NO VACATION FROM DESIRE

was trying to compose something in his head rather than read from his page. Hector, although a wonderful and serious student was also know as a joker and did some funny things at times.

He sat behind my desk. He cleared his throat, and just before he started reading I asked him who he was writing to.

"The Jobs Congress headquarters in Washington," he said, flustered, definitely not trying to be funny. Once he started reading he was smooth and well spoken. "Dear Sir. I'm complaining about the Director of the Salinas branch of the Jobs Congress."

"That's enough, Hector," I said, the class starting to buzz, the intruders perking up their ears.

Mr. Soto, appearing to be the good sport, said, "No. Continue Hector. I want to be criticized. It will help me."

"Si," the poor kid said, looking down at his paper again. He continued reading, "I have been attending the school here for six months. I have learned a lot from all the good teachers here. But the Director brings many strangers into the classroom all day long every day. He makes all the students nervous. They don't want to do anything when the Director comes into the room. He doesn't help us. I wish you could send a better Director here to Salinas."

Mr. Sotos' tough inner political man took over and he stayed remarkably calm. Without another word he brought his group out into the hallway. Then he returned and said to Hector that he'd see him later and maybe they could work out some of the things he thought were wrong. When I was alone with the class again I told Hector to relax because he didn't do anything wrong and he wasn't in any trouble at all.

In the afternoon, because of the Thanksgiving atmosphere, with people stringing and taping decorations on the walls, the discipline I try to maintain when to rest. Most of the people in the class talked quietly in anticipation of having a good time with all their friends at the party.

A student arrived with a note from Mrs. Arroyo, one of our job counselors, asking me to come to her office. Entering the cool green corridor the counseling rooms were on I ducked into the door furthest along. Mrs. Arroyos' small office was divided into two sections by a frosted glass partition. Plants and carpeting reminiscent of offices in the business world were on one side of the partition. On the other side the job counselor was at their desk working, munching on some food a student had brought in from Taco Queen.

Mrs. Arroyo, a forty year old good looking widow, with an ample curly head of hair, who took her job very seriously, said to me, "I think we finally have something for Willy. A one man bookkeeping operation just a few blocks from here. We could send him there now if we could locate Mr. Soto and get his signature. Have you seen the boss around?"

"Not since this morning."

She lamented, "It's tough getting a hold of Juan when he brings the boosters through. It doesn't seem like he's ever in his office. He should leave someone in charge when he goes out of the building. He won't delegate any authority. I didn't want to lose any more time on Willys' case. Now we'll have to."

Stopping a stray student in the hallway I asked her to go to my room and tell Willy Ramirez to please come to Mrs. Arroyos' office. "Tell him Mr. Franklin sent for him. Tell him we have a job for him."

THERES NO VACATION FROM DESIRE

While waiting for the applicant to arrive the counselor made a phone call. "Hello? Mr. Burns? This is Yolanda Arroyo calling from the Jobs Congress."

"Yes. I know I told you I'd be able to send him over today. We didn't have enough time to process his papers yet. It's a very complicated business. It takes a little time.

"How would bright and early Monday morning be? You'll still have him in plenty of time for the holiday business.

"Yes. I'll call you before we send him over. Thanks for being so patient. Goodby."

Willy arrived moments later in a bad mood. I'd never seen this side of him before. His face was dreary with suspicion and annoyance. Both Mrs. Arroyo and myself were smiling at him with the anticipation of the news we were about to give him.

"It looks good, Willy," I said.

"Yes", agreed Mrs. Arroyo. "Do you have a nice suit you can wear on Monday? We have an interview all set for you. You can even walk there from here. I told the hiring manager about you and he said he was interested in someone with your background and experience. What do you think?"

The old man ran his hand over his gray brush haircut smoothing it some. He furrowed his forehead and tapped his right thigh with the middle finger of his right hand. The old hobo said, "Is the job good enough for a man like me? I don't want to just take anything that comes along."

I was shocked by his evasive reply. He didn't seem like he wanted to apply the things he learned at the Jobs Congress to the outside world. "Willy!" I gasped. "This is your big chance!"

"I don't have no good clothes to wear," he said in outright protest to the proposition, folding his arms over his chest, and pouting like a prima donna. "The gray suit you wore on you last interview will be just fine, Mr. Ramirez," Mrs. Arroyo said, her manner and words becoming more stern. "We want you to make a good impression."

"I hope this job is better than the last one you sent me out on," Willy replied with a profusion of hostility in his delivery, seeming as though he'd fight and argue his way out of any job opportunity he was offered. Since he reacted in such a kindergarten manner, resisting joining the work force, I wondered how the Jobs Congress could alter an attitude like that.

"You're just like the rest of the loafers, Willy," Mrs. Arroyo said, becoming irate, holding her stomach, easing her undigested food through. "We set you up with the best positions we can find and you don't even want to go. Why are you coming to school here? You know, Willy, you should've been out of here months ago. People have been trying to be nice to you, and have let you have your own way. Now it's time to go to work!"

"I won't do it," Willy shouted back at her, stamping his foot in a tantrum. I'd never seen an old man react in such an immature way to anything. I was astounded. I didn't know how to reason with him. I let Mrs. Arroyo do all the talking.

"Well, Willy boy," the job counselor continued with her called for badgering. "You better come in Monday morning ready to go to your

THERES NO VACATION FROM DESIRE

interview. If we report your refusal to the main office they'll get rid of you. Then where would you be? No stipend from here and no money coming in from a job. This is it, Willy. You have to go to work. No one is giving you anything anymore." Willy stormed out of the office in a rage. We didn't know what to expect from him on Monday morning.

Chapter 10

It had never been my style to date students, but the pupils at the Jobs Congress were older, and as far as I knew there were no rules about teachers and students not being able to fraternize on their own time. I felt no guilt at this time concerning Lena. We hadn't communicated since the devastating phone call awhile back. We were doing our best to forget about each other.

Rita made herself known to me my first week at the Jobs Congress. After seeing her for the first time, it didn't take long before I started looking for her. Her perfect brown face featured mysterious liquid eyes. Her smile exploded with even white teeth. Her manner of swaying her firm ass as she strut made her irresistible to me. After a little exposure to each other it was very easy making arrangements with her.

She didn't live too far from the high school James was fired from. My cousin found new life playing drums in a band called Dog Face. It was one of the most popular local rock bands on the central coast. James was an area luminary now, and was taking advantage of all the carnal encounters that came his way. He had women over the house all the time.

Since he could change and have variety almost every night he didn't worry about his vow of celibacy anymore. Seeing him getting plenty from the groupies whetted my sexual appetite. It led me to taking Rita to see him play with Dog Face at the Peninsula Community College in Monterey.

I'd been on the elegant grounds of the campus only a week ago when James forced me to go to a comedy film festival. We went on Charlie

Chaplin night.

"You want to laugh tonight?" James had asked me.

"Yeah. Sure. I'd rather laugh than fuck."

"We must have the same brain," James mused. "They're showing some Chaplin flicks at the college tonight."

He heard my protests. "That guy may have been great when he was in, but no old timer like that who doesn't even talk can make me laugh. I don't want to see some played out guy like him."

I was surprised to see the ultramodern movie hall in the Audio-Visual Building filled to capacity with fans. We could only find seats in the first row. We had smoked a doobie on our slow walk to the campus. "He's passé," I squawked to James, annoyed for having to sit too close to the jumbo screen.

"Did you ever see him before?" James asked. "In an entire movie?"

"No."

"Sit back and watch then. And shut up. I don't want to miss anything."

"This was a waste of money."

"Shut up I said."

The lights dimmed in the bowl shaped theatre. The flick started. The audience was oppressively quiet. When Charlie simply appeared on the screen a tidal wave of laughter erupted from the crowd in back of us. James was smirking and on the verge of cracking up.

I watched the clown walk across the silent screen. His presence and mannerisms were so funny that I couldn't hold it in anymore, and burst out laughing. I laughed so hard I had to stop to cough and clear my throat.

THERES NO VACATION FROM DESIRE

The crowd was howling with laughter. It was like taking a ride on a rollercoaster when the sensations make you laugh so uncontrollably that by the end of the ride you're too weak to push back the safety bar. People were stamping their feet and standing up trying to get control of themselves. Words from the screen were unnecessary. The magical tramp went about his business as though no one was watching him. His appearance and antics had this effect on all of us.

When I arrived at Ritas' shanty in the square block development of mean dwellings, a Chicano ghetto, I was aware of the great poverty even before I go to her door. Her beautiful appearance at school, her fine, stylish and expensive looking clothing never led me to believe she lived in such squalor.

All the bungalows were painted gray, and the trimming was white. It looked like the builders slapped them up in a day or two about fifty years ago. Lots of makeshift repairs going on or completed, giving each house an individuality, a personality. An originality shaped by things going wrong, then repaired.

Ritas' house wasn't in the worst condition of all, but it sure wasn't a pretty sight. The outside paint was blistering and peeling. There were broken and cracked window panes. She used an empty flattened box of Cheerios in her small door window to replace the glass. When she answered my knock and looked at me, her face beaming between her long lustrous hair, everything inanimate became secondary. Her looks were so compelling to gaze upon that she negated the rural blighted surroundings.

"You can sit there," she said. "Be comfortable." She led me into a sparsely furnished worn wooden floored living room. Although the furniture was on the verge of dilapidation, she seemed to be a good housekeeper, the place being neat and clean.

She left me alone briefly when her baby started crying. The wails were coming from a room on the other side of the kitchen. She was only gone a few minutes. When I didn't hear the kid bawling anymore I thought well of her mothering techniques, although I have no idea of what she did. When she returned she sat on the couch with me, and said, "My sister will be here soon. She's staying over watching the baby tonight."

This was the first time we were alone together. I was wondering how she felt, going out with a teacher from her school. She didn't seem like a student to me now.

She noticed me looking at my watch, and said, "They should be here soon. Then we can go. We're going to Monterey?"

"Yeah. To see a band called Dog Face. My cousin plays drums with them. Did you ever hear of them?"

"No," she said. "Are they from around here?"

"Yeah. They're very well known."

When I mentioned music she rose and put an album on her record player. "It's The Temptations," she said. "They're my favorites. I like all soul music."

"Me too," I said.

There was a slight sickly knock on the front door. Rita opened it and a young man and woman entered. Rita was relieved they had arrived. They exchanged a few words in Spanish with each other, though Rita changed

THERES NO VACATION FROM DESIRE

back to English very quickly, not wanting to be rude to me.

Rita introduced me to her sister. Maria was a few years younger than her, and not as good looking. Marias' boyfriend Jose, nodded at me with an unconscious innate distaste, which wasn't obviously insulting. The sister and boyfriend then disappeared into a room just off the living room, and closed the door behind them.

I was relaxing, listening to the scratchy sounds of the record player as Rita was putting her finishing touches on, her makeup and stuff. She wore very tight fitting jeans, and a blouse of light color that accentuated her silky dark skin. We sat on the couch again still trying to get comfortable with each other. She didn't mind me smoking a joint, even though she told me she didn't use pot anymore.

"Don't think bad things because my relatives didn't stay and talk with you."

"I didn't think anything of it. Honest," I told her.

Maria returned from the bedroom and joined us on the couch. She lit a cigarette and ran her fingers through her hair. Rita asked her, "How is he?"

"Alright now. He needed the fix. He's alright now."

Rita, still wondering how to treat me, said, with big sad eyes, "Jose is a junkie. He's addicted to heroin." I was stunned by the information, and only nodded my head, not feeling able to discuss what to them seemed like an everyday problem.

Walking over the rolling, slopping hills of the Peninsula campus, among a mixture of buildings both old and new, both Spanish and

American, it seemed we were a million miles away from the poverty stricken shanty town we just left over in the Salinas Valley.

"I don't come to Monterey often", Rita said, smoking a Marlborough.
"No?"
"I've been here with soldiers from Fort Ord that I dated. They usually take me to Seaside to dance."
"I love music but I don't dance."
"No?" she seemed surprised.
"No." I had been out nights to hear Dog Face play in small juke joints and dives from King City to San Francisco. Their distinctive roaring sound, a combination of blues, soul and rock was the pleasure of all those who loved that sound. When they played the bars and had run of the place, and could perform their own material, they always played the hard stuff.

James had told me that the band had been approached by a record company executive from Los Angeles. He was making offers to them to record an album. Something that would give them a shot at national recognition and an opportunity to make a lot of money.

Dog Face had been opening concerts, way before James joined them, for the big bands on the coast, warming up the audience for groups like The Grateful Dead and The Doobie Brothers. James was mingling with a lot of great musicians. My cousin now felt he was doing what he was born to do. Make music. Dog Face had incorporated some of James' tunes into their repertoire.

"It's great getting paid for something I'd do anyway," James had told me.

THERES NO VACATION FROM DESIRE

There were no frills in the well lighted auditorium. The evening was billed as a dance, but from the bands' reputation, and the type of fan attracted to it, it seemed impossible. No one had ever heard Dog Face play dance music. It looked like a clean cut college freshman crowd as Rita and I bulled our way close to the stage.

James hadn't cut his hair since he'd become a professional musician, and was one shaggy dog face. He was wearing black leather pants and a black leather vest with no shirt. His concrete, well defined football body was exposed to all. The lead guitarist and singer had a ponytail to his waist. The bass player wore a white tuxedo, and the rhythm guitarist wore Mickey Mouse ears.

I couldn't believe the mild soppy stuff they came out playing. It sounded like Lawrence Welk on acid playing a Led Zeppelin song. Dog Face was under contract to the college to be a dance band and that's what they did.

All the lights were turned on for a dance, well dressed college kids checkbook scholars, were holding hands and swaying. Rita liked the music and couldn't keep her feet still. She put her hand in mine, which I found very exciting, but when I felt her grip getting tighter as though she was about to lead me to the dance floor, I said, "Why don't you let one of the college boys dance with you? I want you to have a good time."

"I will," she said, continuing to hold my hand. "You're strange," she added, laughing, then walked to where the boys and girls were getting together.

After a few songs I looked around trying to locate Rita. I noticed that although the crowd, upon entering, had been a collegiate type, when I glanced around now the place was filled with freaks and hippies. Dog Face had attracted their true audience to the college.

Rita returned to me a bit winded after a few dances, and said, "They play great music to dance to. So easy to move to."

"If you think that's good you should hear them rock."

"I stopped dancing because it looked like everyone else had." She was right. Although I had been watching James most of the time, keeping the beat, blending with others just as good as him, I also noticed that with the influx of freaks, the dancing had slackened off. Most people were only listening now. Even the people who came to dance.

"Dim the lights," the lead singer Bub said to one of the stagehands. To the audience he said, "I think this is turning into something we didn't expect". He consulted with his band mates, and I could see James smile. Then he screamed into the microphone to freaks, "How does this grab you!". Bub ripped out a blues riff on his guitar that made the hair on my arms stand up. James started pounding his double bass and the band was off, and the hard core rock came pouring out.

The true music arrived. The freaks took out their pipes and joints and the place got heavy with smoke. The bands beat and rhythm were no longer conducive to dancing, except for a few freaks who moved in a contorted jerky style that seemed to fit the music since it was so out of time with it.

Unknown contributors slid out a dozen or so bushel baskets filled to the brim with hard crusted brown bread loaves to the middle of the dance floor. As the wired crowd started congregating around the food, they covered the floor with bodies, bringing the flow of the audience right up to the edge of the stage. The dance became a concert. I lit a joint, and to my surprise Rita smoked it with me. Then bottles of cheap wine were being passed around. It all seemed timed so well I wondered if Dog Face had planned it that way from the beginning.

When the band took their next break I brought Rita to the stage and introduced her to James, and then to the rest of the band. Dog Face lived together in a farm house near Castroville. Except for James, who continued living in Monterey with me. I'd been to the farm a number of times to listen to them rehearse.

While the band was on break the speakers blared dance music. A large part of the crowed moved to it. James, since becoming a celebrity, had changed from not dealing much with people to becoming an extreme extrovert. He danced with Rita when the song "Disco Lady" came on and she told him she loved it.

After the great concert I was approaching my house with the beautiful girl still with me. It was around two in the morning. I was wondering why there was an ambulance in front of the house. I stepped on the gas to get there quicker. There was a commotion going on next door in Ralphs' apartment. When I knocked on the door to find out if everything was alright the Japanese woman answered it.

"What happened?" I asked her, knowing she could understand and speak some English.

"Ralphie sick. Faint. Okay now. Doctor here."

"You need help?" I asked her, dismissing my amorous plans, seeing something more important had to be taken care of.

"No. He okay. Tomorrow."

Without James' drum set in the middle of the living room the place was enormous now. Rita was a little shaken by the medical incident, even though she didn't know Ralph. However, she was more tired than anything else. My plan was to bring her directly into the bedroom. When I succeeded in doing that without any problems at all, I became very excited and horny when I realized I would get my own way with her. We were both dressed when we hit the bed. By the time I was on top of her she seemed to have nodded off to sleep.

"Come on," I said. "Don't go to sleep now."

"Ugh," with a slight snore.

"Come on," I said. "What's wrong?"

"I'm too tired," she said, seeming to fall into a coma.

I started humping her trying to get her started that way, but her battery was so low she wouldn't crank at all.

"If you don't know about it it'll never hurt you." When she didn't respond to that I opened the top of my pants and pulled my stiff quivering cock out. I pushed her face down to make her take a look at it, thinking it would be an eye opener.

When I started pushing her body to move in an uncomfortable position she resisted, like she was awake. She was like a corpse that still had a little life in it. It seemed like it could go through the motions if I could just get it started doing something. I was dying for relief, having now climbed around her body two or three times, was touching and probing her like a medical specimen, was licking and kissing where skin

THERES NO VACATION FROM DESIRE

was exposed, but she was still as dead as a cadaver.

I opened the front of Ritas' pants and stuck my hand down in under her panties, prying my fingers into her cunt. She reacted with a shudder. Nothing else. No resistance, no encouragement. It was like a smorgasbord. All you want for the taking. I dug my fingers deeply into her, and soon she was dancing on her back, though oblivious. Getting my own way with the living dead.

When I started pulling her pants down she wouldn't let them past her knees. I had my hand in her panties again trying for penetration. She suddenly came to, her eyes lit by something close to modesty, saw she was almost undressed, sat up, pulled her pants back up, and layed down to sleep again, leaving me with a neglected hard on.

I waited about ten minutes. When she seemed out cold again I started fumbling with her pants again, which she had left undone at the top. I was determined to come one way or another. My cock grazed her hand as I was rolling over. I thought I had the solution to my problem.

I picked up her hand and kissed her palm. I put her hand on my ballooning cock and I almost detonated in ecstasy. If felt like her velvety little fingers encircled it, and held it tighter. Her hand in mine, her hand on my cock, I masturbated with her hand. Ah, it felt so good and she didn't seem to mind. I kissed the beautiful sleeping beauty on her cheek.

When I awoke in the morning Rita was gone. I don't remember her leaving and I don't know how she got home to Salinas. She left a sulky three word message on the night stand "Once was enough." I felt the same way she did. I rolled over to sleep and enjoyed Ritas' scent in the bed.

Driving to work on Monday morning after a very entertaining Thanksgiving weekend, I was thinking about Willy, and how he would come back from his tantrum last Wednesday. The first person I met upon entering the Jobs Congress building was Rita. She was relaxed and friendly with me. We spoke, and she made it clear that she wasn't interested in me anymore. I was glad to see her in a good mood.

It was getting close to lunch, and Willy had gone on his interview earlier that morning. When he returned to the Jobs Congress he went directly to Mrs. Arroyos' office. Mr. Soto and I were there too. Willy gleefully told her that when he arrived to talk with Mr. Burns, he was informed by the secretary there that the position had already been filled.

"Where the hell were you last Wednesday, Juan?" the counselor angrily said to Mr. Soto. The Director was trying to take charge, but seemed defensive. Willy was sitting next to Mrs. Arroyo, gloating, smiling content that another job fell through and he could remain at the Jobs Congress.

"Mr. Franklin," the Director said with a nasty tone as though he would try and use me as a scapegoat for taking abuse from Mrs. Arroyo, "What is she talking about? Maybe you can clear it up for me."

"No. You're the only one who can clear it up," he was rudely informed by the counselor. "If you were here or had left someone in charge when you left Willy would be working now. Not sitting here with that shit eating grin on his face."

"Please Yolanda," Mr. Soto said soothingly. "This is tough enough without using language like that."

"WELL EXCUSE ME!" she shouted back with mock courtesy, "But I find I can't do my job here because of you. What the hell do you mean to this place?" She was so angry and willing to have it out with him that her intensity startled me.

"It's alright, Yolanda," I said. "They'll be other jobs to send Willy out to."

"This is only the first time it's happened to you, Jack. After awhile you'll be screaming and hollering just like me and not caring who hears it either."

Mr. Soto, trying to cope with the woman's rage finally asked Willy what had happened. The hobo said, "I walked over there this morning. Right after I checked in here with Mrs. Arroyo and Mr. Franklin. I put my new suit on and everything."

"We can all see that, Willy," Mrs. Arroyo said, getting angrier by the second.

"When I got there the secretary acted like she didn't even know I was coming. She said Mrs. Arroyo never called her."

"I did call her damn it!" Mrs. Arroyo erupted. "You see, Juan. You see. You're ruining the credibility of this organization in this town. They lie to us and don't even treat our applicants with honesty and courtesy anymore. They've been let down too many times with late arrivals and no shows. The hell with your politics. You'd better start running this place like you're the Director or Ill find a place where they appreciate my talents." She broke into tears and charged out of the room.

"I don't think there's anything left to discuss in this case," Mr. Soto quietly and politely said to Willy and I. "Before you gentlemen go let me ask you to remain a few minutes, Jack. I have something to discuss with you."

"Sure," I said, as Willy stood and shook hands with the Director. "We'll get something for you yet," Mr. Soto promised Willy.

"I'm ready," Willy acknowledged. "I can't wait to start working."

I sat calmly in the Directors presence having no idea of what was coming. We watched Willy walk out the door. Mr. Soto withdrew a letter from an envelope he had. It was one sheet of paper covered with handwriting. "Is this yours?" he asked.

When he handed me the letter I was taken by surprise, and said, "Yes. That's mine."

I remembered the week before, late, Mr. Soto and I were the only people left in the building. I was making copies on the Xerox machine of a lesson I was giving to my class the next day. Mr. Soto stood on the other side of the lobby getting his mail from the rack. We had a pleasant conversation.

When I got home and couldn't find my notebook in my briefcase, I realized I left it on top on the Xerox machine. Inside the back cover of my notebook was a letter to my parents that I hadn't mailed yet. I wrote them I had a low paying job, and if an opportunity opened up someplace else, I would surely take it. The next morning I found my notebook with the letter still in it, seemingly unseen and unread.

When the Director presented me with my letter to my parents. I knew he had found it and made a Xerox copy of it. Knowing what he did, I didn't panic when he showed it to me, but asked him, "Where did you get this?"

"Oh, someone left it under my door," he said, unsure, like he never

THERES NO VACATION FROM DESIRE

prepared himself to hear that question.

Juan Soto was immoral when dealing with peoples personal lives. I knew I wanted revenge for his unethical betrayal. My position at the Jobs Congress became precarious. I didn't know what would happen to me in the near future.

Chapter 11

James decided to move out of our house. He wanted to live with Dog Face at their farmhouse near Castroville. I told him my relationship with Mr. Soto had deteriorated and I might have trouble holding onto my job. He said, sweetly murmuring Mr. Harrison "All things must pass."

"That's easy for you to say. You're making all the money in the world now. You don't have to worry about anything. What will I do here if I can't afford the place anymore?"

"I'll help you out," my cousin offered. "If you need money for anything I'll give it to you. But don't hang a guilt trip on me for abandonment. I'm just moving a few miles down the road. You can come out every day. You should. You like what we do, right?"

"That's not the point," I said. "What about Ralph? Huh? What are you going to do about him? The woman can hardly take care of him anymore. The guy should be in the hospital but he won't go. Jesus, it took me fifteen minutes to help him up the steps the other day. He said it hurt all over."

James, getting a little annoyed with my attempts to make him feel remorseful finally had enough and said, "You do something for Ralph. You have a car. You can take him to the doctor. I'm just moving along buddy. Don't try and hold me back now. I've been waiting for this my whole life. I'd do anything for Ralph. But for real the guy's dying and for real he knows it. He's looking forward to it. Be careful with that chair when you put it in the truck. You nicked the other one."

Carrying the light chair down the steps to James' pickup truck, just as I was about to begin my descent, there was a knock from inside Ralphs' door. I looked expecting to see the Japanese woman, but saw the ghostly, pasty faced sergeant trying to smile. His facial muscles were shot.

"How you doing, Ralph?" I asked him through the glass. He tapped the pane twice indicating he wanted to talk with me.

"As soon as I bring this chair down. I'll be right up. Just give me a minute." The ghost nodded contentedly seeing his request would be granted.

The chair was the last piece of furniture James was taking. When I placed it snugly on the flatbed of the truck I used heavy rope to tie all the furniture into place. To make sure nothing fell overboard I tied knots that looked like rocks, although they were haphazardly done and I didn't know if they would hold.

Ralph was standing with his hands in his pants pockets near the refrigerator when I entered his apartment after knocking. His speech was a bit slower now. His face couldn't convey his emotions anymore.

"Jimmy's moving out today?"

"Yeah Ralph. Not far though. Just over to Castroville. He'll be able to bring you fresh artichokes when he visits."

"That's great. He hasn't been in yet to say goodbye. When I saw you I knocked on the door. Tell that boy he'd better get his ass in here for a beer before he shoves off. I know that guy. Once he goes today he ain't never coming back."

"I'll tell him, Sarge. I'll send him right in. I'm helping him move into his new place today. I'll see you when I get back in case you need any help with anything."

"God bless you."

A little later James and I were on our way to his new abode. It was a huge farmhouse on top of a hill. The nearest neighbors owned horses. They were breeders.

Driving north, just out of Monterey, we slowed down for a stranded motorist standing next to his burgundy Ranchero station wagon with stenciled WATKINS CLINIC on the front side door of it. James was slowing down to help the guy, then stepped on the gas when he saw the door placard, but realizing he couldn't leave now, said, "Oh boy. One of those guys."

The needy man was so clean shaven it looked like he couldn't grow a beard. He was in his early thirties. He was extremely slender, and wearing a new pair of stiff jeans. He displayed a maniacal arrogant look in his eyes when he spoke, and a docile timid look when he listened.

"You from that sex clinic out near Big Sur?", James snapped.

"Yes sir," was his easy toned, though somehow sarcastic, reply.

"If that makes you uncomfortable why don't you go on your way and I'll ask help from another."

"We're going through Seaside. Get in."

Since talking with Gail on my way to San Jose, I'd always been curious to find out what the Watkins Clinic taught people. How do you teach people to do things they were born to do and enjoy? Why do people have to learn these things?

Like a true fanatic to his cause, the sex professor lost no time with his indoctrination, rather than concentrating on his immediate car trouble. That's when I knew why James tried to speed away when he thought he could escape. The pontificator enunciated quietly and rapidly, and since he could speak about the most common subject in the world, and a subject the common man never mentions unless in a vulgar way, it was fun listening to him. It was humorous hearing him speak about such things in clinical terms. However, once he actually got into his basic philosophy, telling us he had the solution to our problem, it was outrageous.

"We believe all human beings are bisexual," the professor said.

"Who asked you?" James snarled. "No one brought that subject up."

"What makes you think that?" I asked the stranger.

"Don't give him a chance," James said to me. "He's full of shit."

"If you feel threatened by my words," the man said to James, "then this IS the solution to your problem. I know how people react. You're much too uptight, my friend."

"I'm no friend of yours," James said turning, ignoring him.

The therapist was sitting between James and I in the cab of the truck. The first opportunity the zealot had he continued talking about what he thought was right and true. He said, "We believe if a person leads a well balanced sex life that's the key to living a healthy and truthful life in general. We believe that love among men will stop wars."

"What about women?" I asked.

"The same."

"We feel," he continued, "we know it's true, that there is a spiritual duality of male and female in each and every human soul. No exceptions."

"Oh Jesus," James said. "Working out conflict is the key to solving all our problems."

"You're right, my friend," came the voice of the rider. "And the conflict within man is that he's both male and female and the halves don't know how to get along with each other. We're educated wrong from the cradle and by the time we should be happy functioning adults the halves within us hate each other so much that it incapacitates us. It causes mental disease."

We somehow avoided hitting an exhaust system, muffler and pipes, left rusting on the road, causing the truck to swerve severely onto the shoulder, loosening and rearranging all the furniture on the flatbed. We had to stop to align everything a new.

When James reentered the truck, the professor started talking again, offering us a free day of lectures and demonstrations at the clinic.

"How about a free fuck?" James continued with his point of view, not wanting to hear anymore.

Instead of keeping his mouth shut like an intelligent man the teacher raised his voice and hollered, "I'm used to talking with assholes like you! I'm always involved with haters as I try to spread the truth!"

"Spread the truth all you want," James said. "But if you try to spread your legs I'll kill you."

The counselor seemed frightened now. The drummer stopped the truck. The professor said, "The station is up the road some."

"No it isn't, James said. "It's right there. Don't you see it? You better get what you want there."

"Excuse me, sir," the sex prof snarled, continuing with his better-than-thou attitude, "but once you offer help to someone you should feel obliged to follow through on it."

James stared at him, and he finally said on his way out, "You can't speak English to an Eskimo."

Chapter 12

Welcome to Castroville. The artichoke capital of the world, the big sign read as we entered the little town a few miles up the road. Fruit and vegetable stands galore. "We just have to pass through Pajaro Street. Then up those mountains on the other side of town."

"I know, James. You know I've been there plenty of times." We passed a wooden artichoke as tall as a rocket ship.

"I'm calling Randy Grey tomorrow," I said.
"The principal of the Adult School?"
"Yeah."
"Nice guy. I took you to see him once. Remember? We went to see another guy and Randy was in his office. I introduced you to him."
"Right."
"What's up?" James inquired.
"I heard they were opening their jailhouse school again. I want to let them know I'm interested. I think if I call and let them know it would help."
"No more Jobs Congress?" he inquired.
"The sooner I'm out of there the better. I didn't feel bad about calling in sick today. I hate that place."
"That didn't take long."
"It's not my fault."

When we arrived at the two story cigar box farmhouse that was electrified and wired for music throughout, James was in a good mood forgetting about the Watkins Clinic representative. I knew the other guys in the band. It was still too early in the day for them to be cranking anything out through the amps.

They all helped us move the furniture form the truck into the house. When the easy work was done we sat around getting high. After awhile I decided I didn't want to stick around anymore.

"Let's get going, James. I still have a few things to do today."

"Why don't you take the truck then. I'm gonna stay here. This is where I live now. We're going to rehearse soon. Tomorrow's Friday. Why don't you come out sometime. Then I'll give you a ride back to Monterey. I'll be able to talk with Ralph a little more too."

"Okay."

Instead of driving directly to Monterey I decided to go to Salinas to the Adult School office. I wanted to show them I was serious about working for them. Instead of going to see Bill Getz over at the Gray Eagle some night, I stepped into the Adult School office. After speaking with a pleasant young secretary with a big fifties hairdo, I was led to the inner office of Mr. Grey. His first assistant, Carlo Jacinto, was there too.

"Yes Mr. Franklin?" Mr. Grey, wearing a sharp creased navy blue suit asked, extending his hand as I entered his book vault of an office.

"What can I do for you?"

Since the Adult School was more in tune with the realities of the world and not buried in academic overindulgence, and since a practical man was running the show, Mr. Grey was kind to all the people he met.

Randy Grey enjoyed being nice to people. In his office, in place of

THERES NO VACATION FROM DESIRE

a desk was a round table with a glass encased candle in the middle of it. It wasn't lit. The white walls were covered with art works by students and teachers from throughout his multifaceted well run system.

"Mr. Grey," I said, shaking his hand. "I heard from one of your teachers. And I don't know if it's true. That you're about to start a program out at the county jail. If that's the case then I'd like you to consider me as a candidate to work there."

The fiftyish, well preserved principal glanced slowly and deliberately at Mr. Jacinto, and they communicated nonverbally. The second in charge was a professional administrator in his late thirties, wearing a stylish three piece suit. His grooming was perfect. The polish of his being well dressed and courteous, seemed to emerge from the example of the boss man. From the look they exchanged with each other I felt I had discovered a secret that shouldn't have been divulged, and should they acknowledge it?

"Yes," the natty Mr. Grey said. "We've been thinking about it. We've tried it a few times out there before and couldn't make it work."

"We heard you've been doing an awfully good job over at the Jobs Congress", Mr. Jacinto said, "from our language teachers there."

"We were just about to take a ride over to the jail to take a look at the facilities", the top man offered. "Do you have the time to come with us? We won't be very long."

"Sure," I replied, hardly able to believe the luck I'd found here today.

The big beige luxury lined Buick was parked in Mr. Greys' personal spot in back of the office building. In addition to the Adult School, the building also housed the main offices for all the divisions of all the public schools main officials in Salinas.

"Do you have a California teaching license?" the curious Mr. Jacinto asked.

"Yes," I replied from the back seat.

Easing out of the lot in mid afternoon onto West Alisal Street I could see the serene campus of Hartnell Junior College directly across the street. The college specialized in nursing, and there were a lot of women walking around. It had been some time since I rode in a car and they didn't play the radio. Going through the heart of downtown, passing the courts and the small temporary hold jail, Mr. Grey asked me, "Is there a specific way you would do things out there? How would you approach it?"

Thinking back on my experience of working with psycho kids in small street unit schools, I said, "I'd have to see what it's like before I make any fixed decisions. But in general I'd try to individualize it for each student. Maybe learning activity packages. Each student working at his own pace on his own material." The questioners seemed pleased with my answer.

"The inmates have special problems," the principal said, as we cruised by Sherwood Park past the California Rodeo Grounds.

Not knowing anything about prisoners and why they were in jail, I said, "I'll do my best. I'm a fast learner." Their inquiries concerning education were mostly philosophical rather than practical. They were more concerned with the lives of the students rather than with the material.

As we passed the Dunkin Donut place, just past the Chinese Cemetery, along Natividad Road, we entered a complex of a new and

THERES NO VACATION FROM DESIRE

modernly designed municipal buildings. In addition to the County Jail for Adult Prisoners, there were also the Juvenile Detention Home, The Health And Welfare Department, The General Hospital Of Monterey County, and The Department of Weights And Measures. We drove through the official complex of buildings on a newly paved blacktop with yellow speed bumps. The last lot we entered was the one we were looking for.

We were on the outskirts of town and not much of Salinas could be seen from there. There was a beautiful view of the big brown mountains capped by Freemont Peak, the highest point in the range. The spacious parking lot was only half filled with cars. Yellow lines on the blacktop surface indicated the spots.

As the three of us walked across the lot towards the jail we could see through the chain link fence that was open at the gate. Anyone could walk through unmolested. Razor sharp barbed wire along the top of the fence was intimidating. On top of a skinny pole just inside the gate was a television camera so someone inside the facility could always see who was coming and going. Inmates were dressed totally in blue denim, their shirts, pants and caps, along with white socks and black boots. They were engaged with their work details, and as far as I could see were unsupervised and left alone.

"This is a minimum security jail," Mr. Grey said, "Most of these men are in here for two years or less." It seemed if any of the convicts wanted to escape it wouldn't have been difficult. They were sweeping out in the parking lot, and some were trimming the shrubbery around the fence. They all looked at us giving them the novelty of new thoughts.

We stopped at the gate near the camera on the pole so they could get a good look at us. We walked silently and slowly along a spotless narrow cement walkway cutting through a well tended lawn, and finally through a door and into a state of the art facility before we met anyone wearing a uniform.

We were met by a just approaching retirement aged old man. He was wearing thick eyeglasses with modern frames. His rank was lieutenant, making him second in command, subject only to the captains' orders.

Although the lieutenant was superficially courteous, he was not going out of his way to be very helpful. His uniform looked like it was pressed and ironed three times every morning. His polished Department of Corrections badge was displayed proudly on his chest. The pistol in his holster was at his hip. A long keychain dangled from his belt loop and extended into his pocket.

As we stood in the entrance foyer of the building there was another door, which was open, that led into the jail proper. Crossing the threshold of the inner door we were at the point where the uncondemned public meshed in close quarters with incarcerated. A small empty room was pointed out to me by Mr. Jacinto, and he told me they were thinking of using it for the classroom.

"What do they use that room for now?" I asked him. Before Mr. Jacinto had a chance to answer a road crew of alert faced cons, fresh off the highway, entered and waited with us in the hallway. A guard with a shotgun on his hip stood just outside the doorway they entered through.

THERES NO VACATION FROM DESIRE

We stood among the imprisoned as they joked and kidded each other. Just another group of working stiffs on their way home to the wife and kids. They were also wearing the blue denim uniform of the county jail jailbird. Two guards entered the hall through an armored security door from the jail interior. They brought the road crew, a few at a time, into the small likely classroom, to be searched. "Now we know what it's used for," Mr. Jacinto said with a gruesome smile. After being searched the inmates could proceed inside to their dorm wings.

We were no more than a slight diversion for the boisterous cons who gave us the once over, decided we had nothing for them, and went about their business again. Opposite the search room on the other side of the hallway were three more rooms, each separate from each other, though joined with bordering walls. The officers mess was next to the search room.

The lieutenant was in charge of our tour. He had a few words with Mr. Grey, then led us inside the jail. We walked through the opened armored security door onto a cement floor that was flawless and clean. We were in the hub that was the center of the one level jail. Around the hub were spokes sticking out, the wings the cons lived and existed in. There was a dorm wing with beds where they slept, and a cafeteria wing where they ate.

There was a caged unsentenced wing for men who still had to go to trial. They were stored in there because they couldn't post bond or were denied it altogether because for the seriousness of their crimes. Some were waiting to be shipped to prison. Inmates in the unsentenced wing couldn't walk around the rest of the jail. The sentenced had the freedom of access to most parts of the facility. There was one more wing. The one we went to see.

In the center of the hub was an ultramodern superstructure that looked like a grounded flying saucer. Something they borrowed from another galaxy. It was the nerve center of the jail. Dark tinted windows all the way around made the guards within seem like flighty moving martian phantoms rather than solid men.

I was curious to look inside the flying saucer, but the lieutenant led us to a wing just to our right. He pushed open an unlocked door letting us in. We were now separated from the hub by a glass wall with chicken wire embedded in it, which insulated us from the constant din that had no origin. I didn't know where the noise was coming from. It seemed like the building itself was loud. Talking bricks.

The area we were in was very large and impersonal. Plenty of light was coming in through the openings near the ceiling that looked like a combination window-skylight. "This," said the aloof lieutenant, "is probably the space you'll have to use." It was bigger than a basketball court and was sometimes used as an alternative cafeteria for the cons. It could be filled within minutes by unfolding the combination table benches that lined the walls. The lieutenant left us alone in there and he went his way. We had time to talk things over.

"Do you think you could work in a place like this?", Mr. Grey asked. "Do you think you could create a learning environment for the students in here?"

"Yes," I said, unused to the proportions and dimensions of the gigantic space, but eager to get the job and work here. It was a challenge. We wandered around and inspected every corner of the room.

We were rudely treated by a guard in the flying saucer who said over the P.A., "You guys in there." Mr. Jacinto, not sure if they were taking to us, pointed at himself, although not seeing anyone to address in the saucer. "Yeah you," came back with a disrespect for what we represented that seemed ignorant and deep. We didn't know what they wanted so we walked towards the exit, when we heard over the PA, "Hurry up. Move a little faster." We knew they were having a little fun with us. We complied and maintained our dignity with grave faces. There was a line of prisoners waiting to enter the wing to set up the tables so they could eat.

When we arrived back at the office in downtown Salinas Mr. Grey asked me to sit at the round table. He asked again, "Do you think you can work under those conditions? You already got a taste of what it's like. The authorities don't cooperate very much, and it's been extremely difficult trying to get an ongoing program to work out there. All of our attempts have failed so far". Wanting the job I said, "Yes. I have some ideas. I worked well with delinquents in New York. I think I could work with that type here." Mr. Grey smiled as though he knew something that I didn't, and said, "Well Mr. Franklin. I think we'll be having interviews for the job very soon, and you're wholeheartedly invited. You're still at the Jobs Congress, right?"

"Yes."

"We'll get word to you somehow when the interviews will be starting."

"Thank you."

Chapter 13

Hammonds department store in Monterey was stocked with any type of gift I'd ever need to buy. Christmas was close. Walking into the store to a winter wonderland of tinsel and plastic, a type of Christmas atmosphere that many Californians have never experienced firsthand, made me feel at home. So what if it was seventy- five degrees out and surfers were in the ocean. So what if I had to go indoors to find the refreshing cold of Christmas.

It was an odd winter too because the rainy season never started. Just like the weather is cold on the east coast this time of year, it's supposed to be wet on the central coast of California. It didn't happen this year. It was a strange year, an off year, but most people didn't regret it.

By some quirk of fate I had selected Mr. Sotos' name out of a hat a week ago. It was my job to buy him a Christmas present for the Jobs Congress seasonal gala. At first I wasn't too pleased to have to buy a gift for a man I'd lost all respect for, and hadn't spoken to for close to a month. I lost respect for most of the students too. Teaching others to work when they didn't want to was wearing me out.

I wanted my gift to reflect my attitude. I thought I could have some fun with this. The store was mobbed with shoppers buying presents and artificial trees, and all the rest of the paraphernalia that goes along with the Christmas hoopla.

Passing through the hunting section I noticed a glass case with as many knives as it would take to supply an outpost in Vietnam with silent weapons. On top of the counter was a selection of practical jack and pen knives. I thought I might get the chief something along those lines knowing how great a backstabber he was.

Fliking blades in and out, rapping the casings with knuckle shots to see if they were durable, the sportsman working behind the counter asked me if he could help me.

"Maybe. I was thinking of buying something for my boss for Christmas. These knives may fit the bill."

"This is our least expensive line here", the bearded young clerk said. "That's good. My boss ain't worth a shit." The clerk laughed. He priced the least expensive line for me and I decided it was too good for Soto.

It was the first time I'd been in Hammonds. I wandered in leisure trying to find the ideal gift for a boss I didn't want to have anything to do with, and a boss I hoped to be leaving soon. That gave me unlimited reckless freedom.

There were a million and one knickknacks on the shelves of that department. I scanned the WORLDS GREATEST variety, hoping to find the perfect present. The salespeople left you alone unless you were looking to buy over the counter. On the third shelf from the top was a marbly looking plastic gnome wearing a professors robe and mortarboard. The face was pinched and tight like his shoes were too narrow. Written on the pedestal under the grotesque figure were the words WORLDS GREATEST TEACHER. The caption ruled it out as an appropriate gift for the chief.

I scanned the animal kingdom knickknacks hoping to find something there that would appeal to me and end my search for a gift.

THERES NO VACATION FROM DESIRE

Passing my eye over the glass menagerie I perceived the animals looked much wiser than the gnomes. The camel with the unconcerned face with the caption reading WORLDS GREATES HUMP. The tiny chimp scratching his armpit read I'M A BARREL OF LAUGHS I thought would be suitable, until I remembered Mr. Soto had no sense of humor.

I laughed when I saw the skunk with words I'M A LITTLE STINKER written under it. The realistically shaped creature with the demure eyes and painted white stripe on its back was the one I wanted. A sales lady finally approached me after seeing me standing at the same shelf for fifteen minutes and asked, "Do you need any help?"

"Yes. I want to ask you something if it's alright."

"That's what I'm here for," said the little lady who looked like she was a seasonal holiday worker at Hammonds, but worked packing squid at a cannery the rest of the year.

"I really like this little skunk a lot, lady." She smiled and seemed on the verge of answering me, but she checked herself and I continued speaking. "Do you have one around that says the skunk is a big stinker? That would be more of what I'm looking for. If not, this one is okay, but I'd like one that would really stink the place up."

"I'll take a look at our stock for you, sir," she said, unconsciously holding her nose and speaking nasally. She returned moments later and said, speaking with nasal passages cleared, "No sir. The only ones we have are the little stinkers."

"This is fine then. I'll take the little stinker. Can you gift wrap it for me?" I asked, thinking how fine this gewgaw would fit into the Directors' ludicrous collection of these things in his office.

"Sure." She pointed out the cashier to me and said, "When you pay she'll direct you to the gift wrapping window."

The Jobs Congress automotive warehouse hangar was arrayed with Christmas decorations. The festivities were in full swing by the time I arrived. No matter what was going on I couldn't get accustomed to the fact that the weather was warm and it didn't feel like Christmas. My present for the chief was under the big tree in the middle of the floor. A mariachi band was playing joyous music. The teachers and students were together socializing. They didn't have to come back for a week. I was hoping they'd open the presents soon because I had to leave just before two in the afternoon.

I stayed a couple of hours making myself conspicuous. I sneaked out before they opened the presents. I'd been doing a lot of walking lately because my Mercury was no damn good. To walk to the other side of town would take about an hour. I resisted using Ralphs' car even though he couldn't drive anymore and told me I could use it whenever I wanted to. My shoes were becoming a disgrace.

I marched across town giving myself enough time to get rid of the beer swimming around in my brain. I entered a log cabin coffee shop a few blocks from my destination.

There was a little time to kill so I read the Green Pages of the San Francisco Chronicle to get my mind off my impending appointment. I didn't need to review anything. I only needed to relax. When I emerged into the bright afternoon sunshine my head was clear and I was confident.

THERES NO VACATION FROM DESIRE

I'd had enough job interviews in my life to know that people either thought I'd be great or a complete dud. There was no in between. I guess most people would think of me as a failure since I've had a lot more interviews than jobs. When I did come into contact with an inquirer who was "my kind of person" it was always a wonderful session. It's self destructive to work for someone who doesn't understand how I approach life.

Unfortunately, most Americans have such an overwhelming passion for money and the so called rewards it brings that it dominates their lifestyles and makes them sterile and impotent in human relations. I rarely meet people who know they're alive. I'm disgusted living with the superficial profit motive constitution of America.

My journeys end was at the downtown Adult School. It was a wooden box two story building, with an outdoor stairway leading to the second floor classes and language labs. I entered the street level door into a very small, carpeted lobby and was met by a secretary there who asked, "Jack Franklin?"

"Yes. Ready, willing, and able."

She smiled and said, "The panel is still screening an applicant inside. They should be finished in a few minutes. You can make yourself comfortable." I thanked her for her hospitality and took a seat next to a new high circular table covered with magazines.

Before I had a chance to look at one, two men entered the lobby from a rear room and one of them was Bill Getz, the book eating daily surveyor of the organization. The other man was younger than me and dressed shabby, as though he'd seen an ad for this job in a college publication and decided on a whim to try it.

When Bill saw me he looked at his watch and said, "Right on time," and winked, and holy shit, how could they not hire me. I'm an insider already. Bill thanked the recently tested interviewee and told him he would be in touch soon, letting him know the decision of the panel one way or the other.

Bill returned to the back room through a colorful print curtain. I could see and smell cigarette smoke coming through the curtain. I was beginning to sweat, and I opened and closed a few magazines without looking at them. I adjusted and made tighter the knot in my tie. All's well at four in the afternoon, I thought. School was out and the place was as quiet and eerie as a funeral parlour.

Bill reemerged, and in the interim had removed his suit jacket and was in short sleeves. It was Friday afternoon. The sun was streaming in through the front window, and the secretary had just left.

Upon entering the back room on the heels of Bill Getz I recognized Carlo Jacinto sitting at a short rectangular table made of lacquered pine. I said "Hello" to Mr. Jacinto, and he stood up to greet me. I was trying to see who else was in there.

Bill told me to sit in the chair at the end of the table. I was enthralled by a young blonde woman who was staring intently at me, bordering on rude, as though she had know me from somewhere and was trying to place me. I wanted to stare back at that pretty face to let her know I was new in California and she couldn't have know me from another time. She

THERES NO VACATION FROM DESIRE

was introduced to me as Susan Embry, an employee of the Department of Corrections working at the county jail.

Sitting next to Carlo Jacinto, who was wearing a pastel yellow shirt under a double breasted navy blue sports jacket with brass buttons that had designs that were too far away and too small from me to distinguish, was an Adult School teacher. We were using her classroom now. I couldn't place her age because when she smiled at me upon being introduced as Joyce Kyle it took many years off a face I first thought to be middle-aged.

Of the four interviewers I already knew two. That seemed like a big advantage. No reason to get upset here. You're among friends. These people want you. They've know others like you and understand your type.

Bill Getz was running the show and said to me, "We each have our own set of questions for you. We'll go around the table and each of us will take a swat. Then we'll ask some more questions when we finish in turn. If you have anything you'd like to ask or if anything is unclear to you Jack, just say something. We'll get things straightened out right away."

At the opposite end of the table from me was the back of a chair sticking up. If I didn't want to look at anyone as I spoke I could look straight ahead. Mr. Jacinto and Mrs. Kyle were to my right, and Bill and Miss Embry were to my left.

After getting over my first excitement upon entering the room and being able to look around at my inquisitors, I realized that Susan Embry was no older than me. She was so beautiful and proportioned so well she seemed stranded in Monterey County. She'd be more at home in southern

California with the starlets trying to make it big in the movies.

Bill started the interrogation and set the pace for the rest of them. The questions were almost identical to what Randy Grey and Carlo Jacinto had asked me three weeks ago when I visited the jail with them. It concerned methods, procedures to be used trying to communicate with criminal types, and just how serious was I about doing a good job. Three of the interviewers took a half hour to grill me.

Bill finally said, "We invited Susan here to ask you questions too. We asked her to vote along with us choosing a candidate. She's been at the jail for quite a while now, over a year, isn't it Sue?"
"Yes," she said, very serious in tone, though her fun loving face always seemed ready to burst into a smile.

When Susan Embry and I began our session it seemed like no one else was in the room. The first time she asked a question she was looking so intensely into my face she seemed on the verge of making ga ga eyes, and hell, there's no telling if she could've pulled me into something like that. What's such a beautiful woman doing in jail? She has a face that would open a lot of doors. There's no telling how far she'd get if she opened her legs too. James would love to see that. I'd be in jail with her. Not a bad place to be if she could be with me.

"Mr. Franklin," she began with a grave seriousness, as though she was all business, and I respected that, "Did you know that if you're hired we'll have to work together as a team?"
"No. I didn't know that. I thought I'd run the program myself."
"The classroom is all yours", she continued. "I supervise the social

schedule for all the inmates. I'm responsible for supplying them with things to do when they're not in school."

Taking advantage of my freedom to ask questions, I said "What do you do for the inmates?"

"I listen to their problems a lot. They come into my office and talk with me all the time. They tell me things they couldn't and wouldn't say to anyone else. I'd be able to help you with the school based on the things they said about it in private. To improve it. To tell you the truth," she continued without any encouragement, "and the others will back me up on this, I need a strong man out there to work with. I've had to endure the last few teachers they sent there. After a short time they were depending on me to get them through. It was unfair. I think once I get the right man to work with I'll be able to function a lot better too."

I wanted to make a joke, but her earnest tone kept me in check.

When I arrived home in Monterey, taking my first step into the apartment, the telephone started ringing. Calls were rare with me, and I wondered who it could be as I picked up the receiver. A telephone voice I'd never heard before declared itself to be Bill Getz. "Congratulations. We've made our decision and your our man." All I remember doing then was yupping into the receiver like a rebel. I was so relieved, so happy and thankful to have been accepted.

Bill let me indulge myself in the outburst. A few moments later he said with decorum and stability in his voice, "It was Sue that got you in. Carlo and I knew we wanted to hire you before we started interviewing. As far as we were concerned you were the man to beat. However, we were sensitive to the opinions and needs of Sue."

"She thought I'd be good for her?", I asked like an idiot.

"Yes. She felt if she could work with you it would be good for everyone. She picked you. If she didn't approve you wouldn't have been chosen. So once again, congratulations."

"Thanks," was all I could say I was so thunderstruck.

Leveling his voice off, Bill said, "I called you so quickly because I wanted to relieve the tension". It was gratifying to know I was working for an outfit that knew how to treat their employees with respect. "You know we have a problem with Mr. Soto now", Bill said. "Telling him you'll be working with us. That's something you'll have to do for yourself. I don't know how he'll react, but you better take care of that next week even though it's Christmas. He should be in his office. You can call him, I suppose?"

"Mr. Soto won't be a problem. He's expects me to quit."

"One more thing", Bill said. "Sometime next week we'll have to meet to start planning. I have to give you all the books and supplies you'll need. You can start getting your classroom ready to. You don't have to bring in students until you feel everything is in order. You do know that as of next Monday you will be on full salary getting paid for your preparation time."

"Thank you for the Christmas present," I said, ending the conversation.

No sooner had I put the receiver down when the telephone rang again. I put it to my ear after one ring. It was Ms. Arroyo.

"Hello Yolanda. How are you?"

"Where were you?", she asked with friendly familiarity.

"Where was I? When?"

"When we opened the presents under the tree this afternoon."

"You wouldn't believe me if I told you. Why?"

THERES NO VACATION FROM DESIRE

"Why he asks," clowning. "Because I had your name and bought you a wonderful gift. I still have it and want you to get it."

"That's very nice of you," I said. "What is it?"

"I won't tell. You'll have to open the package to find out."

"Then I'll have to wait awhile."

"Oh, don't worry. I'm always in my office. You can come in and get it next week. I'll be there trying to line up a job for Willy again."

"You better get him something he likes this time," I kidded her.

"But Jack," she went on in her peculiar frisky way. "I want to thank you, and I hope I'm the first, for wiping the smile off our leaders face in front of almost everyone he knows."

"Did I do that?"

"Come on you stinker. You know what I'm talking about."

"He liked it, right?"

"He liked it so much he smiled in reverse. You must be brave giving the boss something like that."

"I'm not brave. I'm gone. I have a new job," I told her, letting her in on it. "I'll tell the chief when I come in to get your gift."

"I can't wait."

Chapter 14

The officers mess was next to the classroom. Susan was eating with us today. First time all week. Her office was directly across the hall from the officers mess, and next to the work-release program directors office of Hal Halloway. Hal was sitting across the table from me, rubbing his palms together, and quietly chatting with the captain. Mr. Halloway possessed a round red flinty face adorned with wire framed spectacles that gave him the appearance of a Depression Era Gman.

The final office on the opposite side of the narrow jail entry corridor was the captains'. The captain was top dog at the jail. He was a fair minded, even tempered, distinguished looking man with a full head of silver-white locks, fashioned in the most recent of styles, and very becoming on him. His office was lined with oil paintings and water colors he'd made throughout the years. Mostly landscapes.

I'd eaten a few meals with the crew already, and was about to begin my school program after a few days of thorough preparation. Susan had diligently helped me get ready. If it hadn't been for the rumor that she and the ancient beetle browed lieutenant were lovers I would have made a move on her.

A hangdog remorseful looking inmate rolled in the double decker stainless steel food cart from the hallway. The heavily perspiring t-shirted con prepared the food, exposing it, by removing the metal tray tops off the pans. The hot steaming heavy food smelled and looked good. It was the same grub the inmates would be eating after the guards finished. There was enough food on the tray to feed an army, and that's what this was.

One by one, and according to rank, the eaters approached the wheeled mobile cart, and took as much as they wanted. The cooks had whipped up pork chops and gravy with mashed potatoes and string beans. It was the lightest meal they'd had all week. I filled my plate telling myself not only was the salary great, I'd already bought Ralph's car, but the free lunch couldn't be beat either. I wonder who taught the cons to cook like this? Lemonade nice and cold. Yesterday the fresh baked apple pie was thick and crusty.

I had no problems with the staff when they spoke to me unofficially, but I could sense they didn't trust my authoritative role. They were conflicted about how to treat me. It seemed like they were waiting for the pieces to either fit together or fall apart before making a judgment. Many of them believed you couldn't enlighten the cons.

The sergeant, third in command, was a muscular mustashioned man, who wore aviator sunglasses when walking in or out of the facility. Though the sergeant was a little resistant to me, he was curious about New York City.

"I was there three years ago," he addressed me, "for a jailers convention. We stayed at The Hilton. On the Avenue of the Americas. Do you know where that is?"

"Sure. It's right in the middle of Manhattan. Safest area in town. You should've come out to my neighborhood in Brooklyn," I added, seeing a good place to brag within their macho laughing at fear profession.

THERES NO VACATION FROM DESIRE

"How's that guy Jenkins doing at the hardware store this time around, Hal?" the captain asked the work-release director, instead of keeping me and the sergeant in the spotlight.

"He's been going out three weeks now," Hal answered the captain. "Been back on time here every day. He's had no problem with the other employees. The owner of the store said he may keep him on when his time is up here. He knows a lot about the business. He still has four months to finish up here and a lot could happen by then," he ended with built in pessimism.

"I'm glad to hear it," the captain said, swallowing hard, taking a sincere interest in any man who did anything good.

The bitter faced miserable lieutenant was sitting between Sue and I at the lunch table. He always spoke in a negative and argumentative way. Not many of the officers spoke with him.

"Can you pass me the gravy, Sue?" I asked her.

"Yes. Sure," she said, her tone bordering on intimacy, we'd been working together so much. She handed me the little lantern shaped tin in front of the watchful eyes of her alleged lover. As she was giving me the gravy our fingers touched, we seemed to almost lock pinkies, and although it was unintentional, it was still pleasant. I felt a sharp pain in my left shin and almost dashed my face into my mashed potatoes. I bent over to rub my leg, not knowing what happened. I half stood up with a writhing ashen face. Getting control of myself I said to the staring crew, "I hit my shin on something."

The Spanish con who served us this chow walked around the table picking up the empty plates and stacking them on the lower shelf of the food cart. Sue hardly said a word during the meal.

The men respected her and never bothered her. They went out of their way to be pleasant to her. In situations within the jail proper, they were protective of her. She was everyone's property in this place.

"You been keeping busy this week, Sue?" the captain asked when he realized she'd been silent.

"Yes," she said, with a dreamy smile etched about her lips. No matter what her pose she was a beauty, and I felt lucky to be working so closely with her.

"I helped Jack get ready for the next phase. We want it to work out."

Turning his attention to me the captain asked, "About ready to get the ball rolling?"

"Classes will start sometime next week. This afternoon I'm having the first screening. Sue made up a list of men that are interested. She spoke to a lot of them explaining what we're trying to do."

"How many names do you have on the list?" the lieutenant asked me.

"Eleven or twelve."

"If you find one serious one I'll be surprised," he said, scanning the food cart for dessert.

Charlie Lamons entered the room as though he'd been jogging, his keys jingling, and took a seat at the end of the table. He governed the unsentenced wing. The barred wing that's blocked off from the rest of the jail by a big white sail, preventing the incarcerated within from looking out at the freer members of the human race.

THERES NO VACATION FROM DESIRE

The sail was mounted on a wire at the ceiling and could be slid opened and closed, but was almost always shut. The authorities didn't want the visiting public to see the only remnants of a shackle bound, hogtied, overcrowded method of incarceration practiced by police civilizations thousands of years before our own civilization developed. The men in there were desperate. If they had a chance to escape they would risk it.

"I just came in for a hunk of pie," Charlie said, bulbous fly eyes rolling around his head as though he could see in twenty different directions at the same time.

"What do they have today?" Charlie asked.

"Pecan," said the sergeant as he poured cream into his coffee.

"That's great. I have to eat and run," Charlie said. "Freddy is filling in for me for a few minutes."

There was always an armed guard standing in the unsentenced wing among the jailed.

"How's the zoo today?" the lieutenant asked Charlie. "They nervous or what?"

"Nah. They're on the quiet side. It was a good move sending Conners back to the downtown jail. He disturbed all the men. They didn't like his crime."

"His trial starts the day after tomorrow," the captain said. "They'll just have to walk him across the alley now," he concluded, picking his teeth with an ivory toothpick attached to his key ring that only had a few keys on it.

Charlie Lamons had a keychain at his hip big enough to jam anyone's works. "I can't believe a guy like that fucked his own daughter," Charlie continued, snatching pie and gulping coffee. "Excuse my language, Sue," he said, as though she was his daughter. He continued talking about the recent rolled up transfer. "He's a strange one alright. He doesn't seem like a rapist though. He doesn't fit the mold somehow."

There was a ruckus coming from the hallway. A sunglass wearing guard with a shotgun in his hand, deeply tanned from being outdoors a lot, entered the officers mess, and said, "We got in a little early today. I thought you'd be done eating by now though."

The captain responded casually, "Hold them outside for another five minutes. We'll be finished by then. Then you can use this room to search them. We're making some changes around here for you, Mr. Franklin," the captain continued in his pleasant drawl.

"They usually search them in your room when they bring them in for lunch."

I wanted to tell the captain that the room was empty now and that he could use it if he wanted to, but I was sure he already knew that. Then I realized his words were setting a tone for his crew to cooperate with me, that he wants the program to succeed, that he wants to see some of the incarcerated do themselves some good.

"Sorry to be such a bother," I said

"It's no bother," the captain said. "It's just part of the system now."

I wanted to say "Thank you," but I only nodded to him.

When the road cleaning crew arrived the jailers were silent and began shoveling in their dessert as though they weren't going to be gypped out of one single inch of pie crust. Even the latecomer Charlie Lamons

THERES NO VACATION FROM DESIRE

devoured his pie and returned to the ultra secure unsentenced wing.

As we were rising from the table, Sue approached me and said, "There are three or four men on the road crew coming in that said they wanted to see you. Maybe you could talk with them now. I'll try and locate them for you if you want me to."

"Don't they have to eat now?" I asked, thoroughly ignorant about all the rules and procedures at this house.

"Just a word or two to them out in the hallway could do a lot of good."

"Am I allowed to talk with them while they're being searched? Aren't they scheduled to come and see me?"

"Yes. But there are a few who don't know if they want to go. If you show an interest in them it may be the impetus they need."

The waiter quickly removed the empty plates from the officers mess, stacking everything haphazardly onto the cart. He completed his mission by rolling the cart inside the jail to the kitchen. The road crew was advancing into the hallway from outside. They were told to wait. Discipline was relaxed and the inmates were talking with each other, some laughing, stomachs probably rumbling because the scent of food was still in the air. They were returning from a morning of hard labor, walking and cleaning Monterey County's roads and highways.

As they were being searched I waded in among them and asked by name for the man I wanted to talk with. A boy about twenty years old with long hair that was straight next to his head, but curled at the ends, approached me, and seemed relieved by the novelty of talking with anyone new or different during this twice daily wearisome search procedure. His name was Larry Gann." Yes?" he asked, with a fearless grin across his face, the mug he displayed to any authority figure he came into contact with.

"Do you know who I am?" I asked, unintentionally sounding like an egotist.

"Yes," he said respectfully, though keeping that Smiling Jack grin pasted across his lips. "You're the new teach."

"Yes. Miss Embry told me you were thinking about signing up for the school. She said you weren't sure though."

"I haven't made up my mind yet. I was serving time for something else the last time they had a school here."

The jailhouse school had a notorious reputation for failure among the incarcerated, and I had to fight that image all the time. My first responsibility was to let them know I wasn't there to foster a fiasco. I was ready to turn any inmate down I thought was faking it.

I was learning to read them as well as they were learning to read me. Instinct told me I could never show weakness among them. Every word I said had to be decisive and final and had to be backed up. My only chance of prospering was coming at them from the same place every time. There could be no variation from what I thought was right and fair. I sure was no friend of theirs.

"Did you like the school?" I asked Larry.

"Oh, I liked it," he responded, "but the teacher didn't like us." Once in conversation with a con, once they knew they weren't being set up for anything, they could talk, and talk pleasantly, and even prolong the conversation because it helped to alleviate their boredom. "You mean," I asked him "that the school wasn't too good?"

THERES NO VACATION FROM DESIRE

"Right," he said, relieved, not having to state the obvious to be understood.

"If it's going to be like the last time," Larry continued, "then I don't want to go. I might get myself in more trouble."

As we were discussing the problems of the previous school among the cons, many of them were leaning towards us, listening in. Therefore, I spoke with Larry as though we were advertising to the public, for the benefit of anyone else who cared to tune in. Larry expressed an interest in attending my school. I asked him if he knew any others who may want to come aboard. "I may know some," he said.

It had taken four days of preparation to get ready for the entry interviews. Most of my time had been taken up with hauling books and supplies from the downtown Adult School to the Monterey County Jail, under the shadow of Fremont Peak. I worked often with Sue.

I bought some things I thought were necessary to make the room comfortable. Posters and a calendar for the blank white walls were a must. Sue helped me place the posters on the wall. A giant sized calendar that was taken apart, and each month taped up separately, covered an entire wall. The one side of the room that had windows faced the front of the jail. The parking lot, past the well manicured lawn within the chain link fence looked serene from the classroom window. We had a perfect view of anyone coming in or going out of the facility.

Another wall was taken up by a huge bookcase that held all the materials the cons would need. Most of the inmates seemed to be about my age or less. It was a young man's world.

Once Sue and I finished adorning the classroom it was an oasis in a desert of sterile white and boring beige. Sue thought the rock poster calendar that featured a famous musician each month was perfect. Too bad I couldn't get a poster of Dog Face. I hadn't seen James for awhile with my new job and all his concert touring. We were losing touch. Sue got us through the year by taping Paul Simon on the wall. He was wearing a cap and strumming his guitar, probably singing.

> The mama pajama rolled out of bed
> And ran to the police station
> When papa found out he began to shout
> And he started the investigation
>
> It's against the law
> It was against the law
> What the mama saw
> It was against the law
>
> The mama looked down and spit on the ground
> Every time my name gets mentioned
> The papa said oy if I get that boy
> I'm gonna stick him in the house of detention.

If you give a con a calendar he can entertain himself as well as a navigator can with maps. There was no end to the things they could do, figuring patterns with all those numbers up there. In what is traditionally called the front of a room, but in this case was just another side, were giant sized action photos of motorcycles and cars, speeding and racing and displaying to the prisoners what to most of them would be an ideal lifestyle. It gave them something to look forward to when they got out. Earn your diploma and buy your own car.

"I'm ready for the men now, Sue," I told her, as she sat behind her desk in her cross corridor office looking over some forms she had to process. Her entire room could be seen through a green tinted window from the hallway, making it the only office there that wasn't private. It was a very cluttered lived in space.

Although she was alone, that was unusual, because either her lover, the big daddy lieutenant, or one, or a group of inmates were always in there talking with her. Her stunning hooded blue eyes gave her an exotic Eurasian allure.

It was time for me to make decisions. Two mess hall tables in the classroom were arranged in an L shape. When the places at the tables were filled in with metal folding chairs there would hardly be any space to move around. Even with the few seats that were in place now, with no people sitting in them, the room felt crowded. While glancing through some of the questions I'd prepared to ask the cons I was suddenly engulfed in shade. I looked up at a bald headed con so big I thought he was a monster. With my first glance that ugly, bucktoothed, pock marked face was familiar, but I couldn't place it. He was staring manically at me, but the expression on his face suggested a stupidity so ingrained he should've been wearing a name tag so he wouldn't forget who he was.

"Hi. I'm Mr. Franklin. Are you interested in earning your high school diploma?" He shook my hand so ferociously I thought he'd tear it off altogether. I couldn't determine if his motive was negative, indicative of him wanting to rip my limbs off because of his lack of freedom, or positive, due to his elation that someone not wearing a uniform, and not working for the Department of Corrections, was talking with him. His head was shaved so close I couldn't tell what color his hair was.

"Hey," he said, in a too familiar key, "You look like I know you?"

"What's your name?" I asked him.

"Roy Johnson."

It was the gross, pig loving Loser leader. He continued standing while I spoke from my seat, "This is a high school. This is a place for you to do some work. What grade did you make it through? We'll send for your records to determine how many more credits you need."

"I quit at the end of the tenth grade," he began. "They forced me to leave."

"Who?"

"Fucking principal. Teach got me mad and I fucked him up."

"Are you interested in earning your diploma now?"

He glanced out the front window, the liberty it afforded, rubbed his hand over his slick dome, and said, "If it don't take too long. I've got six months to do. I didn't even do anything. I was framed," he started pleading like a jailhouse lawyer, wanting me to take his side. "It doesn't matter what you did. If you've got more than two months to serve you can enroll."

I had decided not to look over the criminal records and psychological reports of my possible students. Once in jail there street backgrounds didn't have much to do with what went on in here. They were forced to comply with authority. They were bossed and helpless. Almost all of

THERES NO VACATION FROM DESIRE

these guys had hang-ups with drugs and liquor.

As we kept the conversation going Roy drifted in and out of consciousness of what he was doing and saying. He seemed seriously mentally ill. A few times I had to repeat a question just to hear him say "Ah?" again. After his last lapse of awareness I decided to throw him overboard.

The mountain approached me and was about to toss the furniture around, but stopped and leaned over coming face to face with me, and screamed, "It was you! You turned me in! You got me busted! You and that fucker quitter! He's here too! I'm gonna kill you and that James motherfucker! He was too good to be a Loser!"

The sergeant was nearby and heard the ruckus and charged fearlessly into the classroom. I stood in the hallway and watched the muscular sergeant rumble with the monster. Other officers arrived and dashed into the room with clubs drawn and swinging. Roy was handcuffed behind his back, and the guards were swatting him on the head with their bare hands as they led him into the jail towards the barred and sealed unsentenced wing.

I had access to most parts of the jail. I didn't abuse that privilege and the guards didn't begrudge me that freedom. After the disturbing episode in my classroom I knocked on the door of the flying saucer to speak with the lieutenant. When I was let in the highest in command there was the sergeant. It seemed when Sue wasn't around the lieutenant wasn't either.

From the command center I looked out at the entire jail. The sail in the unsentenced wing was pulled back for some reason, and I looked through the fine bars at the miserable living conditions of those men.

"Thanks for the help, Sarge. That guy was nuts."

Sitting at the ultramodern console that looked like a training bridge for astronauts, the cool sergeant said in a comradely way, "I was only doing my job. But guys like that Roy fucker are known out here. He shouldn't have been sent to see you alone. That's the first action we've had out here like that in months."

The other skinny bearded guard in the booth was playing around with a leaded night stick, swinging it around and tossing it like a baton. I was watching the television monitor from the front gate camera and saw Sue and the lieutenant entering together.

"Don't say I told you so," the sergeant warned me, "but you've got an enemy out here. That shithead you talked with never should've got that far. Sue didn't know what he was like. All the guards and officers know what each of these fuckers are like. Most of these dopes are coming through on their third and forth tours. They love it here. But watch yourself. You could've got killed in there today".

I looked through the tinted windows of the booth, through the bars of the unsentenced wing. The dorm wing of the sentenced has beds arranged neatly and uniformly along the walls. There were so many guys in the unsentenced wing awaiting their court dates that the beds were placed randomly all over making it impossible for any privacy at all. The can and showers were near the hub of the jail, and from the booth the imprisoned could be seen shitting and showering. They must've jerked off on the sneak.

THERES NO VACATION FROM DESIRE

Remembering my reason for visiting the flying saucer, I said to the sergeant, "I think I know someone in the unsentenced wing. I can't see him from here though. Can I look at a list of names of the prisoners in there?"

"Sure," he said, handing me the roster. I was blown away when I saw my cousin's name.

Chapter 15

In contrast to all the failed trials and false starts and disappointments that preceded being hired by the Adult School, my success within the system was so fast and so comprehensive that it confused me. After a short time of this triumph I was anticipating the seams ripping apart. The struggle to exist was minimal. This was contrary to all my previous experience in life. I was troubled by good fortune and didn't know how to cope with it.

The odd dry winter continued in Monterey County too. The clouds and rain were sparse and light. We were missing a season. I had been preparing myself for the rains for a long time. The authorities were talking official drought. The farmers in the Salinas Valley were complaining. Store owners that annually profited from the sale of rain gear complained.

The average man didn't seem to mind. The man who has to drink and wash himself with it didn't seem to care that the source of life was getting scarce. The main drought groaners were the authorities, and businessmen that try to control the economy. The sea lions and otters didn't grumble.

The dry weather was preserving Ralph well. The rain caused him to rust like an old bicycle left outdoors. His health improved after hitting rock bottom, being bed ridden, and nursed by his Japanese girlfriend. He had steadily made progress since almost dying. Most days he was in his old position on our sundeck, swilling beer.

"Did Jimmy get a trial date set yet?" Ralph asked me one day.

"Yes. In a few weeks. It don't look good though. There's nothing

I can do to help him either. He's so depressed he hardly ever eats. He's wasting away. I go in there and talk with him every day, Ralph. He never has anything to say. I'm worried about him. All he does is lay on his cot all day and night. The lawyers tell him he could get twenty years and it's killing him."

"Jesus," Ralph came in with a sympathetic drawl.

A helicopter flew over slowly on its way to the local naval station. The pilot was visible in the clear bubble cockpit. Although Ralph knew it was futile, he hollered and waved at him, possibly as a leftover survival mechanism from his time in Korea.

"I always let the guys on my side know where I am," Ralph said.

"You talk like you're still at war."

"I am. It never stopped. You always need buddies to help you out. Don't let anyone kid you. Other than being tough and dry the best way to survive a war is to have friends taking care of you."

"What do you do? Sit out here waving at people who can't see you?"

"Nah," Ralph said. "Most times I just watch. Sometimes I'm back in a foxhole praying for help. I'm praying for friends to help me. When I go to the Naval Hospital on Wednesdays I always stick around and talk with the active personnel there. It makes me feel young and healthy again."

After a couple of months I knew that for my school to survive, since there would always be a tremendous turnover of students, it had to succeed by word of mouth among the imprisoned, rather than by force of the authorities. After only a few incidents with students who tried shirking their responsibilities, the prisoners took the program seriously.

Among the brightest and most promising students, some acted as a

THERES NO VACATION FROM DESIRE

screen for goldbrickers trying to enroll. They policed themselves in the classroom and wouldn't allow anyone in they didn't think should be there. Of course their suggestions were all unofficial, but I usually did what they wanted since they knew a lot more than me about what was going on at the jail. Once a working trust bond was established with a con, at least in the situation I was in with them, it was as true as any union I'd ever felt compelled to comply with.

The school was now an ongoing operation with facets serving the individual as much as possible. Wayne was studying for credits only. He had four months to serve and could only start earning them. He'd have to finish up after being released. He was already asking me questions about attending our downtown Adult School. Tom was writing short stories and sending them out to literary magazines trying to get published. Juan didn't work for credits or write short stories, but wanted the quiet of the room to sit and read in. One inspired incarcerated Salinas native wanted to read through all of Steinbeck. Sue supplied the books.

"Twenty years is what they want to give him?" Ralph asked, taking a swig from the brightly colored aluminum can, shaking his head in disgust.

"Yeah. When the police raided the Dog Face farmhouse they found a ton of all kinds of stuff. They're going for the conviction on Cocaine. They want to make an example of James because he held such a prominent position in town before he started playing in the band. James is the only one they're making much trouble for. The other guys were let off with lesser charges. Pot and things like that."

Before calling it a session and going in to prepare for my next day in jail, Ralph asked, "Now that I'm feeling better is there any way I could visit Jimmy? They know he has no family. Maybe I could go and talk with him?"

"No. They won't let you in till he's been to trial. Only relatives and lawyers can see him."

"Too bad," Ralph said. " I thought if he could see how much I've improved then it might help him a little to hold on. But the law's the law, I guess."

When I arrived at the facility the next morning, carrying stacks of books, and two reels of a movie I wanted to show the class, the captain corralled me and led me into his spacious office. Looking out his window I noticed my room had the same front view of the jail. There as an uproar in the corridor with the work crews assembling, getting ready for the trucks to arrive to carry them out to the roads.

"We've had an accident out here last night," the captain said, and the first thing that went through my mind was that the school was in trouble for some reason, and the amiable captain wasn't letting me conduct classes that day. His walls were sparkling white, and one of his prettier landscapes was of Monterey Bay, out near Lovers Point. I put my baggage on the corner of his desk and sat down hard, ready to hear the worst.

"That cousin of yours, James Reeves, tried killing himself last night," he almost blushed telling me, though dealing with a common problem among the inmates.

"WHAT?" I said, jumping out of my seat, and banging my fist on his desk in response to his most direct and startling statement.

"Sit down!" the captain ordered me, like a slap in the face, as he leaned way back in his swivel chair contemplating the ceiling for a

THERES NO VACATION FROM DESIRE

moment or two. "He'll live. He's next door at the hospital now. They'll be holding him for observation for a few days. He got hold of a piece of metal somehow. Sharpened the sucker and cut his wrists. My night man saw blood dripping from his cot and got help right away. He may have bled to death if my guard hadn't responded so quickly."

"But he's alright now you said?"

"Physically, yes. There's no problem with that. But I wanted to talk with you about him. When a man tries doing himself in like that we have to send him to the jail downtown. Nothing personal. Just the rules."

My mind didn't function properly after speaking with the captain. I found it difficult doing anything. Every word I said was an effort. Leaving the captains' office I waded through the cons who were somberly waiting to hit the road.

Stunned beyond recovery, I blotted out my regular morning visit to the unsentenced wing to see James. My personal problems destroyed any satisfaction I felt from the success of the school. I entered the classroom and turned the lights on, getting ready for the school crew to arrive. Ray Sears showed up early to help me arrange the room for the day. He was preparing to take his final exam at our downtown office.

The eleven other students arrived in a group. Some mornings they were late and I had to go to the dorm wing to collect them. Sometimes they were lifting weights and they didn't want to stop. They wanted to show me how strong they were. They all had their own seats and their own books, and they would all test out at different times, whenever they qualified.

Each and every one of them was working on his own subject at his own pace. The classroom provided relief from the lousy tinny Muzak that continually blares out from the overhead speakers all over the jail. It was also the only group room in the facility where the inmates weren't watched by the guards. The assortment of street fighters, drug addicts, alcoholics, pimps, male prostitutes, robbers, liars, car thief's and braggerts were usually well behaved and the problems were rare.

They sat at their seats and occasionally we'd talk. When anyone needed help with anything I'd sit with them and try to explain to them how it worked. I had lots of problems unraveling some of the more advanced math, but from my meetings with James in the unsentenced wing I'd come across a man with a degree in physics, who was glad to teach me how to solve the problems.

The entire day was spent in self study. The only communal activity, other than a weekly movie, was once or twice a week I'd read short stories to them by my favorite writers. After awhile some of them were bringing me short stories by their favorite writers to read to the class.

Ray Sears once read out loud to the class, but his monotone was boring and the guys started kidding around. When I read to them, sometimes for as long as forty minutes, they were quiet and attentive. I always tried bringing in material they would like, and characters they could see themselves as. They roared with laughter almost every session. Once a guard barged in to check it out because he though we were having a party.

A week or two after James slit his wrists one of the many Spanish inmates I'd seen in the yard approached and greeted me. I had noticed him before. He seemed like some type of leader among the men. He was left alone, but when he spoke the others listened. I had him figured as a bully and tyrant. I based my decision on how the other men avoided him, but responded to him when he wanted them to.

When he began he was soft spoken and seemed gentle. "You're the new teach here?" he asked with respect, wanting to chat, checking me out for some reason.

"I'm not so new anymore."

He was short and stocky, a bull of a man, with the face of a matured male in his mid thirties. His harsh irregular features showed he'd been through plenty, maybe enough to put an end to another man. From an expression he used here and there, he seemed like the hardest rock that could ever be formed, and would do anyone in who would bother him or look at him the wrong way. He'd been in prison many times and had served numerous years. He was addicted to heroin.

"You know," he said, continuing in his tactful way, "there are lots of men here who can't speak English. Mexicans."

"Yes?" I responded, not knowing what he was getting at.

"I'd like to teach them the language. Do you have books I can borrow?"

We were standing in a black asphalt yard with high chain link fencing surrounding it. Outside the fence was the pastoral paradise of the California countryside. Some of the inmates never missed feeding time when a neighbor farmer tended his livestock. Once an escaped hog ambled up to our fence, and the men were delighted and fed it through the wiring with whatever they had in their pockets.

A television camera implanted in the building showed the guards in the flying saucer what the prisoners were doing in the yard. There were a couple of hidden corners where I saw men I didn't know passing around a joint. How they got the stuff in jail I have no idea?

As comfortable in conversation with him as he obviously was with me, I said, "What's your name?"

"Omar Sandoval," he said, enjoying talking. He was a very verbal guy. "I've been back here for a month. I'm serving two years. I have an inside detail. I clean out the toilets every morning and then I'm free the rest of the day."

"I think what you want to do with the Mexican inmates is great. We don't have anything like that. How smart are you?"

I asked him for the hell of it. He took me seriously and responded, " I almost have an Associate's Degree."

"Can't you get work-release and finish up?"

"No. Hal let me try it the last time I was here. I fucked up and scored dope instead. I'm no good on the outside."

Talking with Omar was very interesting and I wanted to keep the conversation going. Curious about how he saw himself in the future, I asked, "What's the first thing you'll do when you get out of here?"

"This is fucked up, man," he said, grinning, not embarrassed, talking from the heart, not wanting to fool me, wanting me to know the extent of his problem, "but my first day out I'll score dope. It's two years away, but I know myself."

"You're kidding?" I answered him, instantly sickened by the

THERES NO VACATION FROM DESIRE

magnitude of his habit.

"Nope," we smiled, but we couldn't look each other in the eye. Omar laughed, showing the tips of his teeth, and said, "If anyone brought the stuff in here."

"In where?"

"Jail, man."

"Yes?"

"If I had a chance to get high in here I'd do it. Even if they added fifty years to my sentence. One pop would be worth fifty years to me."

It was gratifying that Omar chose to entrust me with an honest account of his character. I'm glad I was there for him to unburden himself to. After confiding in me, I let him know that I'd speak with my boss and find out if we could develop a language program for only the Spanish speaking. I made a mental note to call Bill Getz that night to ask him if we could do something like that.

Bill was an ideal boss. He was an absentee landlord who took great interest in the jailhouse school, but followed a strict policy of noninterference.

When he hired me, he said, "All I'll do is explain to you what happened before you got here and what we hope to accomplish now. We'll set you up, give you everything you need, send you help if you want it, anything, you name it. But when it comes to making a go of it, it's your baby. You can call me and let me know how it's going, but if I don't hear from you, you won't hear from me. Unless there's some kind of emergency or problem you didn't expect and need help with. It's sink or swim for you, Jack. You make all the decisions. It's your neck and you have to do what you think is right. We've tried every method possible in our previous experiments at the jail and nothing has worked. Good luck."

Bill was as good as his word. As the months piled up we discovered we'd hit on the right modus operandi. Our relationship turned into a consultation system. We had confidence in each other, especially after some of the inmates had earned their diplomas, giving credibility to what we were doing.

My teaching day was done, but I still had a few things to do before driving to the downtown jail. James had spent more time in the hospital than was anticipated. He had done a tremendous amount of damage to his circulatory system with his severe self inflicted stabs, and had only been transferred to the downtown jail yesterday. When I saw him at the hospital he was always heavily sedated and we didn't communicate at all. He was a zombie. I only wanted to make sure he was still breathing. I didn't even try and guess the harm done to his mind and soul.

While beginning to clean up the classroom Larry Gann and Ray Sears came in to help. I was examining a few documents before starting home as Larry and Ray were picking up the foldout chairs and putting them on top of the tables. "After the search I'll get a mop and slosh her," Larry volunteered.

Larry left to get the cleaning utensils when he saw the road crews pulling up in trucks in front of the facility. Ray approached me, and said, "I went to see the work-release director about going to college." He removed a Hartnell bulletin from this back pocket and pointed out some science courses he thought he might like to take. "Work on my degree," he said. "Mr. Halloway told me if I could get a recommendation from

THERES NO VACATION FROM DESIRE

you he would approve me to go."

"No problem. You got it."

As the road crews were lining up in the hallway to be searched, Larry arrived, rolling the suds filled bucket with a mop stick jutting out from the top of it. He stood around talking with the incoming crew, and shared a cigarette with one of them. After most of them were searched and allowed to return to the dorm, Larry mopped and cleaned the classroom, leaving it spic and span, so no one could complain about it.

Crossing the hallway to Sues office to find some books for James to read, I was accosted by the cranky lieutenant, who had just left the captains office, and had slammed the door on his way out. I usually avoided him when I saw him coming, but it was too late this time.

"Mr. Franklin," he snarled at me, as I stood in front of Sues window, and saw her eating a piece of cake while sitting at her desk.

"What do you want?" I lowered myself to his degrading tone of address. "No schoolboys in the hallway when the road crews come in," he said, seeing Larry roll the suds bucket into the jail. "You got that?"

"Yes sir," I said, mustering up as much sarcasm as I could. "Anything else?"

"Not yet," he said, jabbing his finger in my chest.

"Then get out of my face," I said, keeping my hands to myself, and walking away.

Entering Sues office, she was wearing a quirky smile across her lips after witnessing my exchange with the lieutenant.

"Want some cake?" she asked. "I baked it last night."

"No thanks," I said, very hot, my stomach still churning from my near explosion with the old man.

"I don't think he likes you," she said.

"Where did you ever get an idea like that?"

"Just a hunch."

She was slightly flushed, possibly excited by two men, one her lover, the other a person she loved, almost coming to blows in front of her, knowing it was she they were fighting over. She reached into the top draw of her desk and took out a piece of paper with handwriting on it. It looked like a poem. She said, "The lieutenant wrote that and gave it to me. He gives me at least one a week."

I didn't gloat as I read the sentimental tripe. "Nice," I said awkwardly, wondering what she was up to. I felt that the love that was expressed to her in the poem was being used to tell me she loved me. The lieutenant put the words in her mouth.

After selecting some novels for James to read, Sue and I continued talking on a personal level. It was so pleasant communing with a sympathetic soul that I didn't want to leave. She was the old guys lover, and I knew I wouldn't make any moves because it would cause problems on the job. My work was more important to me than making love to a beautiful woman. She sensed and enjoyed my interest in her, but also discerned my reasoning in this affair.

The sun was out as usual. Arriving at the downtown jail, next to the post office and court houses, I was thinking what I could say to James to help him. To enter the jail I had to first pass through an alley and then

THERES NO VACATION FROM DESIRE

into what felt like a side door, but was the main entrance. The place felt more like an active precinct house rather than a facility for incarceration.

This bullpen was more in tune with the everyday life of the community. The drunk tanks were there, and when someone was brought in off the streets for some reason, they were locked up in here. County jail inmates were relocated here when they broke the rules. This jail was the first stop in the criminal justice bureaucracy for the incarcerated of Monterey County.

In the diminutive entry chamber, the initial guard sits behind a wire mesh cage that reaches the ceiling. The space is so confined and stagnant I didn't want to imagine what it was like behind the walls, and upstairs, where they packed the punks in like monkeys in a zoo.

"Yes sir?" the guard reacted to my appearance. "Can I help you?" He wore the same uniform as the personnel at the county jail.

"I came to visit James Reeves. They moved him here from the hospital. I work at the county jail. I'm a teacher there."

Within the cage, behind the guard, racked on the wall were a variety of chains and shackles and straight jackets, harnesses and bindings, leaded sticks, helmets, all available instantly and for any reason.

"I thought you looked familiar," he said, looking me in the eye. "When I transported prisoners to the County I saw you. Now, what did you say? What was your problem?"

"I want to visit my cousin, James Reeves. I want to give him some books to read."

"You can't see him now," the guard said, not trying to be offensive. "The sign says," I said, pointing to the schedule taped to the wall, "these are visiting hours."

"I know what the sign says. But we had to tranquilize him. Reeves is a real nervous guy. We can't put him in a cage with anyone else. If anyone comes near him he starts fighting. He's out now."

"He's not here?" I asked, surprised, thinking they may have shipped him back to the county jail.

"No. He's here. But the doctor had to shoot him up with tranquilizers to calm him."

"Maybe he should be back at the hospital?" I said.

"The doctor comes here every day. Reeves don't need a hospital bed. He needs some kind of relief though."

"Yeah, well," I said, "you think you can give him these," putting the novels on the counter of the cage.

"I don't see why not. You're one of us. I've heard some good things about you, mister."

"When can I visit him? When will he be awake?"

"Call me tomorrow," he said, writing his phone number on a small piece of yellow paper. "I'm Sergeant Daniels. I'll let you know what's going on and when you can visit him."

Chapter 16

If James wasn't locked up and suicidal things would've been perfect. The school was expanding. Students were trying to get in by hook or by crook. Some were completely misrepresenting themselves, and others were telling their own brand of the truth with half lies in it. Although the mentality of the cons would indicate they wanted in because scholarship was an easier detail than cleaning the roads, it still hadn't happened before, and even the captain said something to me to that effect.

James was rotting out a few feet away from me in the unsentenced wing. His trial had been delayed again because of his suicide attempt. I'd been in to see him every day, but from his lack of response I was thinking the best thing I could do for him was leave him alone and let the course of his feelings run their route and take him to whatever end he had in mind. I couldn't comfort him. I tried my best.

He was wired and ready to kill me when he was restless. The caged beast. When he was inert there was no telling what was going through his mind. He didn't look or talk or try to present himself as himself.

The morning was starting like any other, but the day was a little special. Ray Sears got his clearance from Hal Halloway and was on his way to his first day of classes at the junior college.

"How do I look?" Ray asked with eagerness, entering the classroom I was preparing for the ones he was leaving behind.
"Like an Ivy Leaguer. It must feel good getting out of the blues?", I

said, referring to jail garb.

"And how," he said, patting down his new set of clothing, the conservative black slacks and pin striped shirt.

"How you getting into town?"

"I'm riding the city bus like a free man. Put my money in the slot and take my seat like everyone else. I'll bet they'll be plenty of women around that school?"

"There are," I told him.

Ray walked out as the lieutenant walked in through the front door. The old man's face was severely scratched as though he'd tried to sneak up on a cat. He carried himself in his normal manner, and even though his face was raw with flesh and blood he didn't make any reference to it. His uniform was uncharacteristically wrinkled, as though he'd slept in it.

"Morning," I said, as he absentmindedly passed me on his way to the interior of the jail.

"Yeah. Hi ya Franklin."

I was wondering where Sue was. She was usually in before the lieutenant arrived, but no sign of her yet. This was unusual for her, never being late or absent since I'd been here. It's strange to say, but I felt a loss and was hoping she'd be in soon. I had a type of psychological dependence on her. It was more than looking forward to seeing her every day. Her presence had a soothing effect on me. Recently, I got myself into the habit of going to see her in her office after any explosive or dangerous job related episode.

All through the day I kept sticking my head out the classroom door gazing across the hallway into Sues' office. Every time I searched

THERES NO VACATION FROM DESIRE

her lights were out and there was nothing but darkness on the other side of her window. I hadn't seen the lieutenant since the morning, but I was sure his disfigured face was responsible for her absence.

Although they wouldn't admit it, I knew most of the cons had a dependence on Sue as strong as mine. They missed her. A day without her was as dreary as a jailhouse life could be. Her absence was tedious and bothersome and disorienting. I felt among the class members hatred growing towards the lieutenant for being responsible for taking the small glimmer of beauty out of their lives.

At work days end the class was dismissed at the right time, but the road crews hadn't come in yet to be searched. I took my time cleaning the classroom awaiting the arrival of Charlie Lamons, the unsentenced wing guard. He eventually showed up, and said, "You ready, Franklin? He's waiting to see you now."

"Yeah."

I followed Charlie. As we passed a doorway into the jail we stopped, and Charlie opened a door on his left.

"Wait in there," he told me. "He'll be in in a second." He shut the door behind me and I heard him lock it. The room was so small it could've been a broom closet.

It was a conference room. Cons in the unsentenced wing met with their lawyers in here. You could go from the jail into the unsentenced wing through these two identical consultation rooms, each separate, and each ones interior visible to the other, because they were separated from each other by a glass partition. These rooms could be seen into from the outside too, because of the glass arrangement of the walls.

I was getting claustrophobia waiting by myself. I could glance out and see the guards and the sentenced inmates walking around the place going about their business. One inmate was giving haircuts to anyone willing to sit on his stool. I watched the barber snipping and combing until my meeting started.

The door from the unsentenced wing opened, and in walked Charlie with a denim clad inmate with hair halfway down his back. His eyes were scanning and evaluating, taking in his new environment, readying himself for what would come next.

"Shake hands and come out fighting," was how Charlie introduced us. "I'll be right on the other side of the door, Franklin. If anything happens just holler and I'll be right in."

"Thanks Charlie."

He was very slender, and he was an American Indian. His skin was pale red, his face flat, and his eyes were slightly crossed. The race of the first Americans. He was composed and stoical. When we made eye contact all surface characteristics faded, and I saw he was suffering.

"Charlie told me you were interested in educating yourself," I said.

"Yes," he said. "I asked him if I could see the teacher when I found out there was one here. I need to get my mind off why I'm in here."

He was coming at me with that jailbird subservience that was genuine with these guys, being dependent on everyone for their existence. I could sense he was taking me in a personal direction and wanted the relief of talking about his crime. His approach vaguely reminded me of Omar Sandoval when Omar wanted to teach English to his compatriots, a program we could never get off the ground.

THERES NO VACATION FROM DESIRE

I'd been severe in sticking to my policy of not asking an inmate why he was locked up. That rule helped more than hurt. But Jesse Stormcloud didn't care at all what my policy was.

He wanted to jaw. "They haven't set my trial date yet. I don't know how long I'll be in here. I'd like to spend my time working. It'll help me forget." In addition to thinking about enrolling Jesse, I was also hoping I could expand the school into the unsentenced wing somehow.

"If we can work something out with Charlie I'll be glad to get you started. We'd probably have to work in here," I said referring to the miniature consultation room. I hadn't worked with a con in this way before so I decided to let Jesse talk and find out what he wanted to do. "I didn't graduate from high school. The last five years I've been working at the sugar beet plant in Spreckles." He was about twenty-five. Although I tried talking about the business at hand he steered the conversation onto a confidential plane.

We were interrupted by a rap on the glass window. When I looked the sergeant was holding a telephone receiver in his hand, and pointing to the receiver on the inside, indicating he wanted to say something to me. "Everything all right in there?" he asked, his voice coming through the line so amplified that Jesse could hear too.

"All right. No problems."

He returned to the flying saucer.

"They just warned me about you, Jesse. You must be public enemy numero uno."

"Don't worry about me," he said. "I'm only a murderer." I froze, you could almost call it a blackout, for a moment or two. All of a sudden I was uncomfortable being near him knowing he killed a man. He got caught and was going to be punished, and that's all there was to it. It didn't seem like he'd kill again. He didn't seem like a killer in the first place.

"I slashed a guy in a fight," he whispered, relaying the facts. Although I didn't encourage him to continue talking this way he couldn't be stopped, and said, "I drink terrible. I blank out when I get loaded. I get drunk too much. I killed a man in a fight in an alley in back of a bar. You want to see a picture of my wife and kids?"

"Sure," I said, seeing he was in control, and was going to say what he wanted to, and was going to lead this conversation in any direction he wanted it to go.

He removed a couple of crinkled snapshots from his unbuttoned shirt pocket after lifting the worn flap. Instead of handing them to me he stood by my side and held them as he pointed out the subjects to me. "My wife is white," he said. I'd never lived in an area populated by Indians and didn't know what that customary white reaction to interracial marriages of this sort was. His wife was one of the ugliest women of any race I'd ever seen. "Does she visit you here?"

"Sometimes. She never brings the kids though."

I was interested in this man's plight knowing he was guilty. I admired him for being able to maintain his self respect even though he knew a life of incarceration and abuse was in store for him. I had a high opinion of him for his coolness in the midst of a ruined life. "Yes, my sons," he said, as he saw me smiling at the picture of his brood.

"Those kids look like twins?" I said.

"They are," he boasted. "My boys."

"Listen Jesse," I finally said after letting him direct the conversation up till now. "We'd better get something worked out if you want to get started with your education. I'll get you anything you need. It's your choice. Whatever you want to work on. It's your time. It's precious. Study what you enjoy. Any subject you think you'd like to try?"

"Arithmetic. I need busy work. Can I get a diploma?"

"Yes. Eventually. I'll explain everything to you next time."

Intending to expand the school into the unsentenced wing, I asked Jesse, "If you know any others in there who are interested in this let me know."

Charlie Lamons unlocked the door to the consultation room and I drifted back towards the classroom. I got a desolate pang in my gut passing Sues' dark room. Maybe I'll give her a call tonight. What happened? Larry Gann must've been missing her too since he was standing outside her office like he was lost.

The first crew arrived, all twenty of them. There was a racket in the hallway. They were smoking cigarettes, talking and laughing, relieved that the days labor was done. Exiting my classroom door for the last time that day I saw Larry pick a joint up out of the sand of a knee high hallway ashtray. He was in the midst of the entering crew.

I wasn't supposed to see him I knew, but I did, and he saw me, and so did everyone else, and it was too late. Larry carried out his plan, and said to me on his way inside, "I've been thinking about this stuff all day." He assumed an air that I was in cahoots with him and that I wouldn't snitch. It was the beginning of a difficult dilemma for me.

"Are you crazy?" I said to Larry. "I have to tell them I saw you do this. I have to protect myself." His face was arrogant and defiant. He swaggered away letting the decision rest with me as to what I'd do about it. If I let him go the cons would get the idea they could get away with something like this anytime they wanted to. Word would get out that I didn't have the backbone to snitch. It could ruin the school.

I was in a fog of fear and alert with despair, knowing I had, in front of a lot of people, aided a convict to obtain an illegal substance. I didn't want anyone thinking my program was being used in a system of drug smuggling between the road crews and the inside guys. I even imagined the authorities arresting me for cooperating with the cons in this matter. I was scared shit.

There were no planned official visitors to the jail that day. The big white sail of the unsentenced wing was open. The guards even allowed some of the sentenced inmates to meander close and talk with the unsentenced through the steel barriers. Charlie Lamons let me in after I got his attention by shouting.

"How you doing, Franklin?" Charlie asked, fumbling with the huge key ring dangling from his holster belt.

"Good. Good," I said, not wanting to talk, wanting to get out of jail so I could go home and think about how the setup in the a hallway had come off, and determine how vulnerable I am.

Inside the wing the cots were close and haphazardly placed anywhere. Wall space was prized. The constant noise of talk and worthless human activity overshadowed everything. Unlike the sentenced cons who had a work and social structure to help them through the day, these guys were locked in, cramped, overcrowded, and left to their own devices to find a way to fill in their time. Boredom is the killer here. Boredom breeds the hate plans and the revenge plans. Combine boredom with ignorance and hopelessness and you're confronted with the human condition.

The ragged roughed up musician was snoring up a storm in the midst of chaos. All the windows in the wing were small and near the lofty ceiling. The only light a sleeper has to deal with is from the low wattage high overhead naked bulbs. The lights were never snuffed, so day and night were both bright. You could sleep your life away once you got used to the never ending noon. The habitat kept you exposed and in view at all times. It left you no privacy.

Wearing jail denims, his hair very long, his full face beard chopped and jagged, dreaming the reality away, James looked like an actual hells' angel. A friend of Satan. He had the privacy of a wall on one side. The cot of the next con was only two feet away.

I was about to sit on the edge of James' cot when Jesse Stormcloud approached me with three cons pursuit. "These guys want to go to school. They want in," he said with his gentle voice.

"Can't you see I'm busy?" I snapped, losing my self control among these immature men for the first time since working in jail. I immediately regretted my lapse, and apologized to Jesse.

James came to consciousness and saw Jesse standing over his cot, and from his drowsy state, reacted, normally for this place, shouting, "Get the fuck away from me!" He picked up his boot from the floor and whipped it at Jesses' head, just missing. The boot lodged between two steel bars it was thrown with such force.

Jesse was about to attack James when we heard Charlie Lamons shout from the other end of the wing, "What the hell are you guys doing over there? Any more of that crap you'll both get rolled up and sent downtown!" Jesse walked away warning James he'd better watch out because no one does that to him and gets away with it.

"Fuck off!" were James' parting words.

"What are you doing here?" James asked me, seeming for the first time to have noticed me. "Didn't I tell you I didn't want to see you again? I don't want to see anyone."

Not bothered by his extremely antisocial behavior anymore, I said, " I have something important to tell you."

"Yeah. That's what you always say. The only thing important to me is getting the fuck out of here."

On the verge of saying it, but not quite mustering the courage yet to spill, I said, looking out into the little yard this wing had, "Do you ever play ball with theses guys?"

"Nah. I don't want to have anything to do with these low lives. Everyone is just trying to fuck each other up the ass in here. But what did you come here to tell me?" he asked, in a more reasonable tone.

"Ralph died a few days ago."

He was dead silent. He dropped off his elbow and brought his hands back, behind his head, looking at the ceiling, slowly puffing out air through his pursed lips. His face seemed about to collapse in rage and disgust and helplessness. He didn't try to hide his tears.

THERES NO VACATION FROM DESIRE

His violent mood was completely broken. He looked like a child now living with the death of a parent.

"God damn," he said. "God damn it!"

"You want to know what happened?"

"Yes," he responded, though inert from the burden of sorrow. Then he said, "You told me he was getting better? You told me they were giving him a miracle drug and he was coming around? You told me they were trying to help him?"

"They were. The Navy already shipped his body south so he could be buried in his home town."

"And the woman? Where's the woman?"

"She's fine. She's moving to San Francisco. She has family there. I have a phone number to reach her at."

"What happened?" James demanded.

"Nothing in particular. He was on the road to death all the time. You know how he felt about dying. I know he's the happiest guy in heaven now. We should feel glad for him. Not sad. I believed Ralph. I'm not afraid of dying anymore because of him. Anyway, I guess the drug they gave him finished him off. It was experimental. It was a risk. He knew that."

The general noise of the wing was giving us the privacy we needed. No one was bothering us, and Charlie would let me stay and talk for as long as I wanted to.

"There is one other thing, James. Here, let me open my briefcase." I snapped open the clasp at the top of my worn leather schoolbag and removed a hard black casing with USA printed in gold leaf across the top of it.

"What's that?" he asked, already knowing.

I handed it to him and said, "The woman gave this to me to give to you. Ralph gave it to her to give to you. He gave her everything he owned. He wanted you to have this."

He opened the casing and saw the Medal Of Honor. Inside, next to the award was a long envelope folded over once to make it fit right. "Citation" was the only word written across the front of the envelope.

"She told me to make sure to tell you to read the citation. It comes with the medal. Ralph requested you read it," I said, as he lifted the medal from its casing exposing the five pointed bronze star suspended from an anchor. The center design shows Minerva repulsing discord. A pale blue ribbon long enough to allow the medal to be worn around the neck was at the top of the award. Over the medal, on the ribbon, was the center pad with thirteen white stars.

"It's a beauty," James said. "He showed it to me a long time ago. Before you got here. I forgot how beautiful it was. It must be worth a lot of money?"

"I don't know. Read the citation. That's the most important thing. He always told people he won the medal but never told them how. Read it. You've been honored. You won the Medal Of Honor. The owner thought you worthy of it."

James opened the sealed envelope, Ralphs' death forgotten for the moment as we investigated the life of the living medal recipient, our friend and neighbor. "What the hell could Ralph have done to win this? Such an easy going guy. When did they send his body down South?" James asked to fill in the time he was opening the seal.

"Yesterday. Read the citation. He'll be alive again when you read it."

"All right. Take it easy."

"Medal Of Honor Winner – Akers, Ralph J., Pfc., USMC."

THERES NO VACATION FROM DESIRE

When James looked up he said, "Ralph was only a private? Shit, he told us he was a sergeant."

"Maybe he got a promotion after he won this? Read on."

Company B, 3rd Battalion, 7th Marines
Place & Date: Korea, April 2, 1952
Entered Service: Birmingham, Alabama
Birth: New Orleans, La.
Citation: For conspicuous gallantry and intrepidity at the risk of his life above and beyond the call of duty while serving as a radio operator of Company B.

"Is that all?" I asked him. "Don't they say what he did? I'll bet he sent a radio message that saved a bunch of guys?"

"There's a lot more. Keep quiet." The jail was gone now.

In action against enemy aggressor forces in Korea on April 2, 1952. With his platoon pinned down by a numerically superior force employing intense mortar and artillery, small arms and grenade fire, Private First Class Ralph J. Akers requested permission to leave his radio in the care of another man and to participate in an assault on enemy key positions. Fearlessly charging forward in the face of a murderous hail of machine gun fire and hand grenades, he initiated a daring attack against a hostile enemy strong point and personally neutralized the position killing two of the enemy. Unyielding in the face of heavy odds, he continued forward and singlehandedly assaulted a machine gun bunker. Although painfully wounded, he bravely charged the bunker and destroyed it, killing three of the enemy. Courageously continuing his one man assault, he again stormed forward in a valiant attempt to wipe out a third bunker and boldly delivered point blank fire into the aperture of the hostile emplacement. Private First Class Akers, by his personal valor and aggressive fighting spirit, inspired his comrades to sweep, overrun and secure the objectives. His extraordinary heroism in the face of almost certain death reflects the highest credit upon himself and enhances the finest traditions of the United States Naval Service.

We were speechless, and thought of Ralph with unbounded respect and reverence. After a prolonged silence James declared, "I can't keep this. They should've buried him with it. It doesn't belong to me. He earned this and he should've been put in the hole with it. I can't take it. I don't deserve it. I don't want it".

"He gave it to you," I said. "Do him the honor of accepting it. He thought the way you live and try to be free was the same bravery as his. He saw himself in you. He loved you. He thought you earned it. That's all that matters. He was glad he had someone to give it to instead of taking it underground with him. I'm leaving it with you. It's yours."

I was walking through the parking lot when a speeding car streaked in and skidded to a rubber burning stop. There were three or four men in it. Visitors of all description disembark at the jail, and I didn't think much of it. Ray Sears jumped out of the back door and walked towards the jail. I'd forgotten all about him and his first day of college.

He was staggering. His new Ivy League clothing was shabby and soiled. It looked like the world had beat him up his first few hours back in it. As we approached each other I expected him to blurt out all the details of his first day back in the mainstream.

THERES NO VACATION FROM DESIRE

"How you doing, Ray?" I asked, as I noticed the car he rode up in roar away. Ray nodded at me, then kept on walking.

Stacking my belongings into the back seat of my car I realized I'd left a pile of papers inside that had to be worked on that night. I locked my car up and reentered the jail. I also wanted to ask Sue something before I remembered she didn't come in today.

It didn't take long to figure out that there was some type of commotion going on that was a little bit out of the ordinary. Three guards were standing in the corner of the hallway and Ray Sears was among them. A few strands of hair were carelessly falling across his forehead, but he didn't care. His hands were cuffed behind his back. When it hit me that Ray had gone out and got drunk with his friends instead of going to school, my first instinctive spontaneous response was to laugh at him instead of becoming enraged by his treachery.

When these men from the world I live and work in got an ounce of freedom they abused it. They didn't know how to live. They were shackled to their impulses. They had no control over themselves. They were no good to themselves and I learned they weren't any good for me either. They're stupid and have no resources to enlighten themselves. In this world there's no vacation from desire.

Chapter 17

Arriving at the jail in a sweat the next morning, determined to speak my mind and tell Larry that I wouldn't say anything to anyone this time, but if something like that happened again I wouldn't hesitate to snitch. With the formation of this plan, as meek as it was, and full of invitations for future problems, it still gave me a feeling of taking control of my own fate.

I was trying to recover from a restless night of sleep. The first thing I did was glance at Sues' office. The light was still out and she was nowhere in sight. The Lieutenant was there going about his morning routine. He had some kind of medical procedure done to his face. It was patched.

There was an eerie silence all over the jail that morning. The silence, combined with an almost sleepless night, dreaming dreams I couldn't remember but found disturbing, added to my nerve-racking distress and anxiety even more.

James was incarcerated and suicidal, and I feared I'd be in the same situation soon because of the drug smuggling episode with Larry Gann. Ralph died. Sue vanished under mysterious circumstances and I didn't know if I'd ever see her again. I lost interest in the jailhouse school once it succeeded, and I hated the environment since discovering the entrenched corruption of human nature within the population. I wanted to quit my job and go back to New York. I would never abandon James. I was his only family.

The Captain quietly entered my room as I was preparing it for the day. He appeared unusually tired with bags under his eyes. His uniform wasn't as sharply creased as it usually is. He was always the first to arrive in the morning, supervising the changing of the shifts from night to day. He sometimes disappeared for long amounts of time during the day, but he had responsibilities at the downtown jail too, and no doubt spent lots of time there coordinating plans with that commander.

I found his rare presence in my room so alarming that while writing some sentences on the board I noticed I'd spelled a few simple words wrong. The Captain said, "We've got a very big problem here, Jack". I was terrified and imagined the guards waiting outside the door with handcuffs ready to roll me up once I admitted to the Captain seeing Larry take the drugs out of the ashtray. They must've caught the stupid bastard smoking the joint.

"Don't look so scared, Jack," the captain counseled, crossing his legs in a feminine way, sitting behind the table at one of the students place. "You're not guilty of anything."

"I'm not scared, Captain," I said, stuttering over my last word, having to repeat it two or three times to get it right.

"Yeah. Okay," he said, forcing a grin. "Whatever you say, Jack. But we've got to talk about something that went on in here yesterday."

"Yes sir."

"Let's go into my office. We'll have more privacy there."

The lowlife Gann will be sitting in there. He'll have his finger pointing at me as soon as I walk in. He'll sing and make up the words as he goes along. He'll pin me with a charge and swear to it and try to wipe me out.

THERES NO VACATION FROM DESIRE

The Captain opened the door to his office by sticking his master key into the lock and turning it a half jigger to the right. There can't be anyone in there if it's locked, I encouraged myself. The room was very bright in spite of the fact that the drapes were still closed. But the whiteness of the window coverings seemed to add to the brightness of the room.

As the Captain approached his desk, sticking his key into his pocket, I scanned the walls, looking at his paintings, and wishing I were in a museum instead of a jailhouse office with a commander. When I took a seat in a comfortable chair with arms I noticed the Medal Of Honor on his desk.

"Where's James?" I asked, forgetting my bogus fears for the moment.
"That's the problem," the Captain said. "Do you want a cigarette?"
"No thank you."
"By the way," he continued. "Did you know Sue quit here as of yesterday?"
"No sir. I didn't know that."
"It was a personal thing you know," he said, leaning back in his swivel chair spewing clouds of smoke into the air, figuring how he was going to tell me James tried killing himself again.
"That's too bad, Captain. I really like her. She was great at her job. Is she coming in to clean out her desk? I'd like to see her again."
"No," he answered. "I got word she already left town."

He stood up and opened the drapes by pulling a cord near the wall, , letting in streams of light , and allowing me to watch the world go by as we discussed grave matters.

"You know what this is, don't you, Jack?" he asked before sitting down, glancing at the most conspicuous item on his uncluttered desk.

"Yes sir, I do. Anything you want to know about it I'll tell you."

"You know what I'm going to say to you, right?"

"Yes sir. Is he back at the hospital?"

"Yes," he said, confirming what I already knew. "He'll be out by this afternoon though. But he won't be coming back here. After a first attempt we observe them for awhile, and if they're all right we mainstream them again. After a second attempt we consider them chronic suicidal and we never let them be. If they're under our control we watch them. We don't want to be responsible for any unnecessary deaths."

"It's a good thing I've got alert people working for me, Jack. It's a good thing my man noticed yours was missing and walked out in the yard. You know what he saw?"

"No sir."

"We've got some Polaroid shots of the incident as we were taking Reeves down off the hoop."

"The hoop?"

"Yes. He tried hanging himself from the basketball hoop."

I hollered out something unintelligible, losing control of myself, irrationally thinking I wanted to shed James and his problems for good, almost (God forgive me) wishing he were dead, freeing me from the burden of his mental illness. If only I didn't have a crazy man to take care of. The responsibility of carrying him was killing me.

As I freaked the captain sat back and let me go through it. He didn't

THERES NO VACATION FROM DESIRE 221

talk as I was wringing my hands, and an occasional stamp of my foot caused his heavy wooden desk to shudder. Thumping out his cigarette in a small plaid bean bag ashtray on his desk, he said, "I'm not going to show you the pictures even though I know you're going to ask. But I'll tell you it was a very gruesome sight. Very bizarre. My staff called me up at home. I've been here since three this morning. You don't mind if I shave now, do you?"

"No."

He inched his swivel chair a foot or two in back of his desk. He leaned down and all I could see of him was his rich and ample silver hair. He produced an electric razor. He also erected a small round table mirror. He spoke as the razor hummed.

"That's some medal there, Jack. I was trying to think back if I'd ever seen one before. And in all my years I don't think I have. I've never met a man who won one either. I was mighty surprised to see it in the wing. Do you know Pfc. Akers?"

"Yes. I did. He was my neighbor. He died last week."

"Did your cousin know him?"

"Yes sir. He knew him well. He knew him longer than I did."

The Captain continued with the hard facts, "My man found him strung up with the Medal Of Honor around his neck." He sat back to let that sink in for a moment or two, and the only thing I could think of was that the ribbon was made of such strong stuff it could hold a man up. "Of course," was all I could think of replying.

"He had the medal ribbon reinforced with a piece of rope. I don't want you feeling as though it were your fault either. He would've used the rope without the medal. He's determined to kill himself. We can't let him out of our sight. When he gets out of the hospital this afternoon we'll isolate him in a cell downtown, and try to keep everything away from him that he could kill himself with."

"Can I take the rest of the day off, Captain?" I asked, feeling sick and queasy.

"I'm not your boss, Jack. You can do whatever you think you have to. As far as I can see you're your own boss. That's one of the reasons you have so much freedom out here. If you'd been another type, a dogooder or reformer, I would've instructed my staff to keep you at a distance. But you work well with these men in distress. You run a hell of a jailhouse school. And don't you know that a program like yours gets me a lot of credit with my superiors too? So do whatever you think you have to today. If you want to see your cousin in the hospital you have an open door. Is there anyone else who could help Reeves?"

"No. I'm the only one who cares."

"You know you made a mistake leaving this in there with him, don't you?" he asked, looking at the medal.

"Yes."

"I don't want to harp on it, and as far as I'm concerned you were doing what you thought best to get your cousin through the worst time of his life. I especially admire you for breaking the rules to do something you knew was right. Don't tell any of my men I told you that."

"No sir."

"Now, and you don't have to take my word for it, Jack. But I'm military, and since this medal has no owner right now I suggest you keep it. You may not think I have the authority to say this, but I have the sense to know when someone deserves something. I'm not afraid to admit to

THERES NO VACATION FROM DESIRE

you that even though I didn't know Private Akers, when I read his citation, seeing the type of man he was, I was extremely moved. That citation is the most powerful document I've ever read."

"He was an even a better person than the citation says he was. His death may have spurred James to try and kill himself this time."

The Captain never mentioned Larry Gann, and that was a great relief for me. I remembered my prized student came in drunk yesterday, and I asked the Captain about Ray Sears.

"Forget about Sears, Jack. He can't get along unsupervised. He'll commit some felony before too long and be sent to the joint. It would probably be good for him. A smart guy like that in prison could earn all types of degrees. Maybe even a law degree. He can't function on the outside though. He's had chances before this one too. Forget about him. He's typical of the type of man we hold in here. They're too weak to take care of themselves."

The road crews were out on the job and the jailhouse was about as quiet and peaceful as it ever gets. The only men around were the ones with the easy inside details, and the guys getting ready to go to school. I decided to inform my class that I wouldn't be in today, and that they had the day off.

It wasn't unusual for me to enter the dorm wing where all of the inmates lived and slept. I'd had many conversations there, both during and after school hours, with members of the class, and others who just wanted to talk. I was accepted there since the cons knew I wasn't there to spy.

The dorm was a long wing with the heads of the beds placed against the walls. There was a very wide center aisle conducive to most social activity, such as weight lifting and watching television.

A footlocker was on the floor at the aisle end of each bed. The footlockers were always locked because these guys stole from each other. They had to protect themselves from themselves. In addition to their footlockers they also had their own upright metal lockers next to their beds. Everything was subject to inspection at any time by the authorities. Some mornings the cons came in tired because of a three AM search. But the guards didn't do that too often.

"Morning Teach," came calls from individuals among the condemned. Some called me by my first name. Some called me mister.

"School's out today," I said at a conversational level to a gathering of students watching The Beverly Hillbilly's on television. They were elated. They were as happy as a group of fifth graders getting the same news. They also knew the reason school was out, the jail being in an uproar last night when James tried to kill himself.

The Hillbilly's departed and The Real McCoy's arrived, as I got the unofficial chatter on what went down last night.

"They had a big time yesterday with the rollups too," said one of the inmates. "They got Sears in the afternoon." I already knew about that one. "They got that white hating cross eyed Indian asshole last night too. Around the same time that shit with your cousin happened."

"What Indian?"

"That Stormcloud motherfucker. If he gets a wiff of booze he goes berserk and tries to kill every white guy he sees. I was surprised to see

THERES NO VACATION FROM DESIRE

you in the conference room with him yesterday."

"He seemed alright."

"I guess. Without whiskey. I don't know what set him off last night though?"

I remembered the harsh words Jesse exchanged with James in the unsentenced wing yesterday, and figured that was the reason he went wild. "They stopped that flatfaced prick just in time. He had his red hands on some sleeping guys throat. That happened a little before they found your cousin."

"They rolled Stormcloud up?"

"And more. He was bleeding like a pulled tooth when I saw him."

The longer I was around these men the worst I felt. I'd had enough of them, and learned as much as I could from them. I felt as demoralized and disheartened and defeated as when I hightailed it out of New York for the green Eden of California. Instead of finding love I was besieged with hate and death.

There didn't seem to be any peace or happiness for me anywhere. This experiment seemed to be over. I don't know if the knowledge I gained was worth the price I paid for it?

Chapter 18

In the office of the Adult School principal Randy Grey, I was giving him reasons I decided to get out of jail and go home to New York. No explanations were necessary though since there were numerous articles in the Salinas and Monterey newspapers about James being murdered by an inmate named Jesse Stormcloud at the downtown facility.

I had some reasons to stay. Investigations were pending. Town officials were clearing things up so they could exonerate their own men. Killings of this kind were fairly common in jail, so not too much pressure was being exerted by the police inquisitors on their own.

James had put himself in the way of death. It was an easy way to commit suicide. Arrange for your own death by another. James' record was public, his recent suicide attempts were taken into account, and since Stormcloud was already up for manslaughter, this killing didn't make too much of a difference to anyone officially involved.

Although initially I was overwhelmed with grief, I gradually began to recover my spirits. The natural relief of James' death, combined with leaving the jail, and now, with the great compensation of Sue coming to New York with me, I had mixed feelings of profuse sorrow and immeasurable happiness. The severity and shock of James' death reignited my desire to acquire love and peace in my life. I couldn't think of anything else to do.

My experiences among the condemned had changed me wholly. It had given me a true perspective concerning the lives of men. There was nothing I could do to change the flow and direction of humanity, but I could change the progress and intention of one man. I lost my will to live among the misfits and oddballs. The streets, fighting, and the oblivion of intoxication no longer fascinated me.

Sue had called me when she read about James in the newspaper. Contrary to what the Captain told me, Sue still lived in Salinas, though she had moved from her apartment and was staying with an old friend.

"I called to tell you how sorry I am about your cousin," she said, breaking the ice between us for the first time since she had left the jail, after nearly scratching the face off the Lieutenant.

We discussed James' unfortunate life for quite awhile, then she said, "I'm leaving for the east coast in a few days. I was wondering if you could tell me of any nice places I could stay at when I get to New York? I've never been there." Already having formulated my plans for the near future, I jumped at this chance to get to know Sue better, and said, "I'm driving in your direction next week."

We got stuck on each other at the jail, had learned to live with each other, learned to depend on each other in most situations. In freedom we didn't know each other so well. We'd become so accustomed to just seeing our way through the chaos of incarceration, that our separate, internal survival systems bound us to each other out here too. Now we had the opportunity to unite under benign circumstances, and help each other down the road.

Driving off the Monterey Peninsula for the last time on the morning we began our cross country trek, Sue told me her plan was to become an actress in New York.

"But you're from LA. Why not stay there?"

"I want to act in the theatre. Shakespeare is my cup of tea," she said, blushing, wondering if I'd ridicule her for her highbrow tastes.

"You don't say?"

Although we agreed this would be a buddy-buddy trip, sharing expenses but not beds, there was a feeling of romance between us. We'd been so filled with sick souls and suffering beings, that to talk about those days, which only just ended, was the furthest thing from our minds. We were still too new on the loose to jeopardize the liberated feeling that came with it. To talk about the jail would bring us back there. To talk about James would be too painful. To talk about the Lieutenant would expose her false security while not knowing how to survive.

"What about your old girlfriend?" Sue asked, as we were leaving the Bay Area, recently having driven over the San Francisco Bay Bridge into Oakland, onto Interstate 80. Interstate 80 would eventually take us over the George Washington Bridge into New York City.

"Just one road all the way," I said, not answering her question.

"One long straight road all the way," I said again, then, "We lost touch. That love burned out. Nothing but new things for me. You know we're making a stop in Tahoe?"

"What for?" she asked, surprised, though delighted.

"I've got friends living there. We're from the same neighborhood in Brooklyn."

"Tahoe is beautiful place. I've skied there."

"I don't think you'll be able to do that now," I said, breathing in the sizzling air of a San Joaquin Valley day.

When we arrived in Sacramento I was impressed by the physical beauty of the city. It was the first time Sue had seen the state capital too, and she marveled at its appearance. We shouldn't have been so surprised though. California is a geographical paradise. The state has all the exterior makings to harbor a contented citizenry, but it lacks soul. It's a superficial Garden of Eden. It's dead. It's a museum of the present. A serious lack of culture exists. Maybe the sun is too hot. I'll blame it on the sun.

The main road that encircles Lake Tahoe is also the main thoroughfare of the village of Tahoma. The entire settlement consists of a general store, a laundromat, and a small ancient motel. Not even a gas station. Immediately off the main road is nothing but forest. Throughout this timberland the locals built their houses. I called Sam's number from a pay phone at the laundromat, and when Sheila heard my voice, she said, "It's about time."

"I'm just passing through, Sheila. I'm on my way back home. My California life is over."

"Where are you calling from? I'll give you directions to the house. Sam is out gathering wood for a fire tonight."

"I'm at the laundromat. Fire? It's hot as hell today."

"It won't be tonight," she warned me.

"I've never been on this part of the Lake," Sue said, admiring the lushness of the forest, the covering, the security of it. "We always stayed at the main motels in Tahoe. All the skiing facilities are there."

We got off the major road, and I was trying to remember Sheilas' directions so we wouldn't get lost. There were a few small houses scattered about here and there along the gravel roads.

THERES NO VACATION FROM DESIRE

Sam and Sheila's house was isolated, located in a small clearing in the pit of the forest. There was nothing there but the house and trees. There was no need for fences or locks. You couldn't see another house no matter what direction you looked in.

When they heard the tapping of my motor, two huge dogs charged off the front porch of the wooden cabin and approached us, surrounding the car, one on my side and one on Sues. They were wagging their tails and barking friendly tones, so amiably, they seemed like our own. They howled with good feelings at the sight of people.

Sheila came out of the house holding an infant in her arms. When she saw Sue she hesitated for a second, since I didn't say anything to her about Sue, but she readjusted immediately and waved at us, and said, "Welcome pilgrims. You've found your way". The dogs were yapping and whooping and seemed almost human in their antics to attract attention and be stroked. Sue grabbed my hand as we walked towards the cabin.

"Beautiful place," I said to Sheila, noticing how fine she looked after not seeing her for years.

"Sam built this house from scratch," she said, "Carpenters couldn't find work back in New York, but they can take care of themselves here."

"It looks it," I said, eyeing the sturdy cabin with two levels, and all the modern electrical conveniences built into it, outside lights and all. After introducing Sheila to Sue, I said, "When's Sam coming back? I can't wait to surprise him".

"Any minute."

The baby boy was fast asleep as we entered the cabin. Sue was taking it all in, not saying much. The dogs had thoroughly checked us out and had gone off into the forest. Maybe to greet Sam.

The interior of the cabin was as rustic as the outside. Although modern in all its accommodations, cooking and heating appliances, it still felt like a throwback to pioneer times. The walls were varnished intricately patterned hard wood. Wildly colorful Indian blankets and rugs were scattered around. The stone fire place was half filled with wood.

Sam stomped in as we were beginning to drink our coffee. He was wearing muddy boots and overalls. His hair was to his shoulders. His thick full face beard was grown to his chest. I'd never seen his freaked out hippie look. The last time I saw him he was clean cut and sanctioned by society. If I didn't know it was him I could never have guessed.

"Jack!" he said, flinging his worn cap onto the antlers that were attached to the wall, then hugging me.

"Hey!" I said, "You never did THAT in the city," surprised by his overzealous greeting.

"This isn't the city. We live differently here, buddy. There's no one spying and judging you here. This is MY place and we like to have friends by. It took you long enough to get here. Is that your Bug out front?"

"Bought and paid for."

"You're sticking around for a month or two I hope? How's things in Monterey? Who's this?" he asked, noticing Sue.

I introduced them, and Sue said, "Jack and I worked together at the county jail in Salinas. He's giving me a ride to New York. I've never been there".

THERES NO VACATION FROM DESIRE

The dogs moseyed into the house through the front door that was left opened. They sprawled on the thick rug near the table we were sitting at, and where Sam was beginning to clean out some weed.

"I'm glad to see you're still at it," I said, indicating the plastic bag he was taking the seeds and stems from.

"Oh yeah," he chimed. "It's still a lot of fun. I don't believe any of that crap the government tells us about ruining your health with it."

After we smoked, Sam put a Rolling Stones album on. LET IT BLEED. From speakers hidden in the walls GIMME SHELTER blasted out. You didn't have to worry about disturbing the neighbors here.

"Let's go outside and pitch horseshoes," Sam said to me, "and let the ladies get to know each other. Is that alright with you, Sheila?"

"Go on. Get out and I'll start supper." Then looking at Sue, Sheila said, "Just relax. It's tough being on the road. It must've been odd spending so much time in jail? I don't know anyone who's ever been there."

"Then I'll tell you all about it," Sue said.

I thought we'd be leaving the music behind as we walked out a side door of the house, but The Stones were even louder outdoors than indoors. "I'll bet you never heard a bird making sounds like that," Sam said, pointing up a tree at a speaker housed in weatherproof casing. It was like we owned the forest and filled it with the loudest and best music we could come by.

Next to the musical tree was a sandpit with a metal pole at each end of it. There were six or seven horseshoes scattered about the sand in the pit. Sam called the bigger of his two dogs over, and said, "Two cans of BUD, please." The hound dashed into the house, apparently understanding what Sam said, and within moments came thundering out again with two cans of beer dangling from his snout in the plastic remains of a six pack holder.

"How's that for a smart mutt, Jack?" he said, gently tapping his dog on the head, then sending him off with a "Scat now" clapping his hands.

"Why didn't you let him open the pop tops for us too?" I asked.

"I didn't teach him that yet. But I will."

Sam went in the house to put on another record. When he returned we resumed our game. He tossed a ringer, and said, "Are you staying a few days? We have plenty of room. Plenty of food too."

"We're only planning on staying the night and leaving in the morning. The money's tight. We have to get cross country with what we have. After seeing this place though I wish I never had to go."

"Don't. We'll build you a house too. Living is cheap here if you know what you want. If you know how to entertain yourself."

"I'd consider it at another time. I'm committed to the girl there for now. She has her plans too. I don't want to disappoint her."

"You know her from your job? At the jail? You know, Sheila and I were planning a few times coming out seeing you. We've never seen that part of the state. But when the kid was born there were so many things to do."

"You should still try getting out there someday. It would be worth your time to see it. It's as beautiful as here. Only different."

"So you and Sue are good friends? You planning on sticking together?"

"We're not counting on anything except getting back East together. It seems like fate is keeping us together though. We helped each other a

THERES NO VACATION FROM DESIRE

lot through that jail trip."

"That sounded like a good job when you wrote me about it. Money and everything sounded good."

"Yeah, it was good," I said. "I learned a lot from it. I was good at it too. But after getting used to it I lost interest in it. Once I knew I could handle it, I was only there for the money." I never told Sam about my heartache over James.

I threw a horseshoe, knocking off Sams' leaner, and making one for myself. "Nice shot," Sam said. "It didn't take you long to learn how to play this."

"It was the Bud that did it."

"So what's back in the city for you?" Sam asked.

"I don't know," I said, watching him toss a horseshoe, knocking off my leaner, getting a ringer. "Beat that," he smiled with satisfaction. While taking up my position for my next toss, I said, "I only know what I don't want. I only know I want to get home."

"Sue have anything to do back there?"

"She's an actress."

"Maybe you could live off that?"

"You must be nuts."

"HOWBOUT A BUD," Sam screamed at his slumbering mutt, and once again, when he heard the magic word, the dog tore into the house, this time returning with one can horizontally in his big mouth. As soon as Sam popped the top he said "BUD" and the beast sprinted inside, then again he reappeared with another can in his mouth.

Sam had great skill pitching horseshoes, and it was his way to let me win a little before he did his best to beat me, which didn't take much.

Walking in the house, dusky out now, the temperature plunging, Sam said, handing me a quarter, "When you pass through Reno play the number 7 slot machine at Gilberts. I always win a pile from that one. It works every time."

"Thanks," I said.

After a delicious supper it got so dark outside that if you didn't know the terrain you may as well stay in, because you wouldn't get very far. The dishes cleared, the fire blazing, we began talking about the remainder of the journey.

"The best way to cross the desert," Sam said, "is at night. It's way too hot when the sun's out. It'll take you all night too. Your best bet is hitting the desert very late in the afternoon. Six or seven. That way you'll get to Salt Lake City while it's still dark. Check into a motel and sleep. You'll need the rest by then. When you wake up the toughest part of the trip begins."

"What's more difficult than the desert?" Sue asked.

"The Rockies," was Sams' straight and simple answer.

"Once you get through the Rockies you got it made." Sam continued. "It'll be a coast for you. The Great Plains. The farm belt."

"Once we get that far I'm home," I said, reminding Sam that I once lived in the Midwest.

"I've never seen the Rockies from the ground," I added.

"When you get to Salt Lake City you won't be able to miss them," Sheila said. "They look like a wall. It looks like someone put them there to prevent you from continuing. You'll look at those mountains and wonder how you'll ever get over them. I'm not lying to you. We went camping in the Rockies for a couple of months before I got pregnant.

THERES NO VACATION FROM DESIRE

We had a jeep and it wasn't too bad. But like Sam said, once you get past the mountains there's nothing but flatlands all the way to the east coast. Right now is the most dangerous part of your journey."

We stayed up late into the night talking, not knowing when we'd get to see each other again. Just before turning in, Sam said to me, "Once you get east of Reno don't bother calling me for help. You're on your own."

"Thanks a lot," I said, as he handed me the sleeping bag which I spread out in front of the fireplace. Sheila made up the couch with sheets and blankets so Sue could sleep on it. After zipping up the sleeping bag the two dogs curled up with me. It was a two dog night.

The way to Reno was a very pleasant ride through mountains in a northeasterly direction. We hit the gambling Mecca about three in the afternoon. We were on the edge of the desert now, as we cruised slowly into the town. The temperature was ninety-six degrees as recorded by a digital thermometer on a bank clock.

A night town, arriving in Reno in midafternoon is like seeing Times Square in the daylight before the neon is turned on. Impressive, but not at its best. Not knowing anything about the town we decided to go directly to the casino and hotel area.

"We'll take the whole town in first, Sue. Then we'll park somewhere and try a few of the one armed bandits. If you see a place called Gilberts let me know."

"Is it a casino?"

"Yes. And that's where we'll make our fortune."

"Whatever you say, dear," she said playfully.

With our newcomers glance the town looked glamorous and inviting and fun. We entered on Virginia Street. Harold's Casino was to the left, and Harrah's Silver Dollar Club to the right. The decorative arch over the street spelled out RENO. Under the name of the town, it read THE BIGGEST LITTLE CITY IN THE WORLD. The Truckee River wound it's way through the middle of town, and if you lost all your money to chance you'd be able to float out on a raft.

We found a spot to park. Elated by this oasis, we found it a great place to unwind before venturing on the most difficult part of our journey, through the desert and then the mountains. It was a pleasure to walk around this little hub of activity sporting about as tourists.

"Gilberts Casino was up that street," Sue said, as we walked hand in hand along Virginia Street.

"We'll make that our last stop," I said, taking Sams' lucky quarter from my pocket. "This is the one and only coin I'll use. This is the lucky one."

We decided to eat a big meal in one of the hotels. When we saw a sign for a discount dinner at the Mapes Hotel we entered. The surroundings were elegant. Our dusty road clothes didn't seem to make any difference to anyone in there. As long as you were eating or gambling no one cared about anything. With all of our needs fulfilled we decided to make a walking tour of this beautiful resort town.

Our exuberance at being in such a famous place, in surroundings so suggestive of wealth, was diminished as we walked slowly through the streets taking in the close up life of the citizens. What we saw was typical of a gambling center, and that my friend, was gamblers.

THERES NO VACATION FROM DESIRE

They were lurking in the hot sun, and in the shade of the marquees. They came in every size, sex, shape and color. You could tell at a glance they were lifelong losers. The seedy clothes they wore combined with faces ravaged by hopelessness were the giveaways. Sue and I had a few hours to kill here waiting for the desert to cool off. We took our time and looked thoroughly at everything. "This place is horrible," Sue said. "These people are making me sick."

"Get used to it because when you get to New York Reno will look like a health farm. I want to play that lucky quarter. Let's go to Gilberts."

Quick steeping back along Virginia Street we stopped off at Gilberts Casino. The doors were big and wide open. It didn't feel like you'd passed from the sidewalk to the casino, except for the air conditioning. Being early, the place wasn't crowded. Every type of gaming table you could think of was there. Card games, dice games, wheel games, you name it.

The slot machines were in a separate room from the tables, and were a world unto themselves. Even if Sam hadn't given me the lucky quarter I still would have taken my turn in here.

"I want to try too," Sue said, in a gamblers flush, thinking she could make more money to help us get back east. She was so enthused about being a big winner she forgot about the men we'd seen in the street who had nothing to eat, and if they could only get their hands on another coin it would give them another chance to hit the jackpot.

"Aren't you going to watch me play the seven with this coin?" I asked Sue.

"Yes. Then I've got some quarters I want to gamble with too."

The machines seemed ostentatious and untouchable, until you put your money in. I was surprised how easy it was to pull the handle down. Nothing to it. "Well I'll be damned," I said to Sue, thoroughly disappointed with my first attempt at casino gambling.

"Give me a quarter, will you Sue? Maybe one of my own will work."

She handed me a quarter from the stack she had in her hand, and before long I put out my hand to her again, then again, and she kept feeding me quarters, until finally I'd spent all her gambling money.

"You used them all up," she said, frustrated, taking some bills from her purse, beginning to walk to the change booth for some more quarters so she could have a turn too. By the time she returned I had found a few more coins in my pockets and was plocking them into the #7 as fast as I could, gently pulling down the well balanced graceful lever with the light touch. In all we lost just over twenty dollars by the time we walked out of the casino. "I don't know what came over me?" Sue said. "I thought I could win a bundle."

We departed Reno about six in the afternoon, just as we planned. The barren inland beach started at towns edge. The sun was still out, though sinking fast, and we had enough light to see some sights we'd never seen before. The terrain was flat and straight, and once the sun was gone, the atmosphere was cool, perfect for my four cylinder air cooled motor.

It was forbidding and hair raising crossing the desert at night. I was glad to have company. I was honestly happy I couldn't see the surroundings as we hummed along in the little spitfire Bug. We kept putting one tire in front of the next, and after many hours we started seeing signs for Salt Lake City.

THERES NO VACATION FROM DESIRE 241

We arrived in the Mormon capital about two in the Morning. We were so tired and hot and disoriented from the desert trek that we stopped at the first motel we saw within the city limits. It was the first night Sue and I slept together. We got a good nights sleep, and in the late morning we were totally refreshed and ready to continue.

A meal, and gas for the car was all that was necessary. We'd been on the road for three days now, and the weather had cooperated with us every inch of the way. This day seemed to be no different. Not sightseeing now, anxious to be off, we drove around looking for a gas station without taking in any of the famous sights.

We didn't have to go very far on a street wide enough to be a runway when we came to the Mobil sign. There was a diner next to it, and we thought we could take care of all of our needs there.

"Fill her up. Regular," I said to the neat middle aged man who was servicing us.

While pumping in the petrol, he said, "I noticed you've got California plates. Long trip?"

"Yes. We're going as far as you can go. We're going till we run out of land. In that direction," I said, pointing at the threatening sight of the immense Rocky Mountains that were looming in the near distance.

"You'd better get some shocks in the back then, mister. You're riding so low it looks like your tail will fall off if you hit a rut or something." At first I didn't believe him, but when I got out and inspected, I could see how low she was, and I told him, "Put in a new set. Will it take long?"

"I'll have it finished in half an hour."

"See you then," I said, opening the door for Sue so we could eat breakfast at the diner.

As you leave Salt Lake City, eastbound, you can see the Rockies in your path. I was thinking that this part of the trip could turn into something physical. The mountains were extraordinarily threatening. A colossal barrier. They were a natural warning to turn back.

Sue and I hardly said a word to each other since leaving Salt Lake City. We were very comfortable with each other that way. The scenery and beauty of the surrounding was so awesome that staring at it said all. There were moments when I wished I didn't have to concentrate on driving so I could look about, the way Sue was. She was easy to please.

Ever since we left the Mormon city we'd been climbing. For fifty miles now, and no relief in sight. As we were approaching the hamlet of Coalville I heard a loud clunk from the rear of the car, where the motor is. Sue heard it too, and asked, "What's that?" though she didn't seem alarmed. "I'll bet that guy didn't put the shocks on right. I'll bet a shock came loose." We kept moving at the pace we'd established, and everything felt fine. I was straining my ears to determine if anything major had gone wrong with the motor.

The red generator and oil lights lit up on the dashboard, and the forward momentum of the car slowed. Sue stayed quiet, sensing big trouble, letting me go about solving it to the best of my ability. The loud clunk had registered in my mind, that, combined with the further actions of the machine, led me to believe she blew up. She sucked a value as

THERES NO VACATION FROM DESIRE

they say.

When she completely died she still had enough momentum to get us to the side of the road. Sue and I got out of the car as soon as we stopped. Sue remained mute, anticipating the worst, not wanting to make it any more difficult, not wanting to overload my thinking apparatus. I winked at her.

At least it happened in a beautiful spot. I walked towards the motor compartment at the back to make an inspection, to see if it was something minor, some loose part on top. We were on the crest of a mountain, on flat ground. Off to the right, in a gully, was a small lake. The peaceful green of summer surrounded us. Birds were chirping in their mountain tree homes. Yes, a very beautiful spot for it to happen. I was thinking, "Other than my girl I don't know another soul in this time zone."

Chapter 19

Sue approached me to ask if there was anything she could do to help. "I don't think so," I said, knowing the machine needed a new set of iron guts, hoping I had the money to match the price. 'I think the worst thing that could happen happened to us," I told Sue. "When the valves go it makes a lot of people give up on their own. Junk it."

"What will we do?" she asked, not particularly stressed, but with a tone of adventure. I felt that way too, but not to her degree, because the dollar signs kept getting in my eyes. If I did have enough money to bring her back in life, we'd have to travel two thousand miles breaking in a new motor.

I made a hasty scan of the motor, too nervous and jittery to even move parts around. "We may as well get her to the shop. I know I can't fix her."

"Will it take a long time to get repaired?" Sue asked, not accustomed to dealing with such major problems.

"If it's what I think it is it could take a day or two. If not, who knows?"

We locked the car up and waited on the side of the road for another vehicle to come along. We were on an Interstate, and traffic was regular, though surely not heavy. We could see a car winding down the road towards us. I stood as close to the highway as I dared, put my arms over my head, and waved him down. A fiftyish couple in a big white Buick sedan with Wyoming cowboy license plates eased to a halt right in front of our car. As the driver was getting out from behind the wheel he eyed the broken Volks, and knew what we were going to ask him.

"How's things?" he asked, not trying to be funny.

"Not too good right now. Got some troubles. Could you give us a lift into town?" As we stood on the shoulder talking, a few cars zoomed past on the Interstate. The mans' wife stayed in the Buicks' passenger seat. The old cowboys' tone was serious though not grave, as though he'd been in these situations himself, knowing they were miserable, but also knowing you may as well do what you have to do calmly, because to do it the other way would be a waste.

"Sure partner," he said without hesitation, like a good Samaritan.

"Coalville is just four miles off the next ramp. I come this way all the time. Got everything you need?"

"Yes. I think so," I said, feeling for my keys, not finding them, then looking in at the ignition of my locked car, seeing them dangling there. The sunroof wasn't locked, so I climbed in through there and got the keys.

After driving the little vibrating Bug for so many days and hours, riding in a luxury car felt very safe and secure. Once this fiasco is over, if I ever take to the road again it would be in a big car. The man smoked a big cigar and was jovial without being offensive at our expense.

His wife asked where we were from, and Sue said, "California. We're going to New York". When the women started talking I lost interest in everything. I started feeling sorry for myself instead of thinking of what I should do next.

Although it was a very warm day, the man turned off his air

THERES NO VACATION FROM DESIRE

conditioner and opened his window half way when he relit his cigar.

"We're coming back from Reno," he said, dumping some ashes from the end of his stogie out the window. Coming off the Interstate ramp, the road was narrow and colorful, and alive with small wildlife.

"We were in Reno yesterday," I said.

"Any luck?"

"About as much as we're having now."

"It looks like you're on a hot streak," he said. When I didn't answer him, he said, "We hit it good this time. Made way more than the gas money back and forth. We go to Reno at least one weekend every month. This time we stayed a little longer. We go to gamble and see the shows. There's nothing like that in Wyoming."

It didn't take long to get to Coalville, and it didn't take long to see it in a glance. The gas station was at the end of the village we entered at. Exiting the Buick, the man and his wife wished us luck. We thanked them for helping us so much.

Approaching a white washed shed with two gas pumps out front, selling a brand I'd never heard of, I was looking for people. There were none at the station, and when I looked along the street of the town I didn't see any life there either.

"It looks like no one lives here?" Sue said, with a touch of desperation in her voice.

"There has to be. There's a big sign on the Interstate."

A very tall man emerged from the shed wearing cuffs up to his ankles, exposing well broken in work boots, and said, "You folks looking for something?"

"My car broke down on the Interstate. It's near the lake on the crest. I guess I need a tow?"

He scratched the back of his neck, spit a streamline into the dirt, and said, "We don't do no mechanical work here. You'll have to go back to Salt Lake City. What kind of car you got?"

"Volkswagen."

"Yes sir. You'll have to go back to the city."

"Do you have a tow truck?" I asked.

"Certainly do," he replied. "The boy is out with it right now. He should be back anytime. We can tow you to Salt Lake then."

"How much?" I asked, almost cringing.

"A dollar a mile."

"How far is it?"

"Fifty miles."

"Fifty dollars?"

"Yes mister," he said politely, "that's what it will cost you."

Chapter 20

After a very expensive two day stay in the Mormon capital we figured we still had enough money to make it to New York if nothing else went wrong. We were once again mountain climbing in the Rockies. We'd gone forty miles and the car seemed sound. The first landmark we wanted to pass and leave behind was the actual spot of our breakdown. We only had ten miles to go before we got there.

If we can only make it past that lake in the gully we'll make it all the way to New York without any more problems. We're climbing that steep grade where I first heard the loud clunk and thought it was a broken shock absorber. "Nothing yet," Sue said tensely, as we got closer and closer to the crest of the grade.

Now we're going past that beautiful serene lake where it happened.
"Is it still there?" I asked Sue, keeping my eyes on the road, thinking a jinx would hit us if I got a look at it.
"Yes. If we didn't break down here I'd say it's one of the most beautiful places I'd ever seen."
"You're one of the most beautiful places I've ever seen," I said to her, turning the radio dial, coming up with a country-western station being broadcast out of Wyoming.

I needed the rest of the trip to work out and end my paranoia forever. I needed to be, and was, crushed into oblivion to save myself. I could now live with the consequences of my actions, of uniting with Sue, of making it together. It was obvious to us by now that we didn't want to separate. This final phase of our trip, taking us to a place where we could start our life together, still needed the binding of rejecting anything negative that could come from it.

You can't imagine how relieved we were crossing the state border and hitting the town of Evanston, Wyoming. It was as though we'd just emerged from a never-never land, a place where nothing is real except horror. We were out.

We were required to get a little maintenance done to the Bug before we could pass into Nebraska. The mechanic in Salt Lake told me to get the valves adjusted and oil changed, somewhere between three and five hundred miles. Sue scanned the Wyoming map and saw that the town of Cheyenne was at the far eastern end of the state, a few miles from the Nebraska border. It was a large town and sure to have the type of mechanic that could do the work we needed done. So Cheyenne was our goal for the day.

Wyoming is extremely scenic. We were encompassed by near and far buttes and mesas. Some of the mesas in the distance looked as large as a state itself.

We had to vary our speed until we got a valve adjustment. We weren't making good time. I felt I might be too tired to drive all the way to Cheyenne, and we started looking for an alternative plan.

Sue wouldn't drive on the Interstate and wanted me behind the wheel all the time. We stopped at a roadside coffee shop where you could ride a horse in a small corral for three dollars. We decided over a meal to try and drive to Laramie by nightfall instead of Cheyenne. Laramie

THERES NO VACATION FROM DESIRE

was fifty miles closer.

Reaching our Plan B destination at dusk we saw the big blue illuminated V W sign as we declined off the Interstate ramp. It was just a few blocks off the highway. We could sleep in town, get the car done in the morning, and that would end our maintenance obligations for the remainder of the ride. When we hit the Great Plains sometime tomorrow, the Bug will be fine tuned and frisky. The breaking in would be completed, the new parts formed and fitted.

We got a motel room in the heart of Laramie. If you go a few miles off the Interstate the rooms are as much as fifty percent cheaper. I wanted to sleep in this famous old west town for historical reasons too.

I couldn't stop thinking about the cowboy era here. When buffalo and Indians were all over the place. I wanted to walk around and get a feel for this town which is so representative of the American west of times gone by. As Sue and I were taking our luggage from the Bug trunk in the motel parking lot I gazed into the street and thought about some of the people who may have roamed it.

Laramie is thoroughly modern now. It's a twentieth century town with all the present day conveniences that the rest of the nation enjoys. The old timers would be shooting out your tires if they had a gripe. Wyatt Earp must've been here. Jesse James. General Custer was a candidate. Wild Bill. I guess I could've dreamed of them all. I pictured a gun fight out in the street next to the sign that read INTERSTATE – FIVE MILES.

My imagination went on a cheerful binge, free from the constant danger of my car exploding. Our room was a wild rooten tooten cowboy bunkhouse. It was decorated with antlers and fringe curtains, with buttes on the wallpaper. It was like a kids bedroom.

Sue and I showered together washing the road grime off each other. Refreshed and comfortable, feeling great for the first time since leaving Reno, we layed on the cozy bed with an imitation cowhide bedspread on it. We turned on the television, smoked a joint, and quickly fell asleep. I awoke about four in the morning and discovered the television was still on When I returned to bed Sue asked me where I had been.

"I never left."

I arose early, but Sue wanted to sleep some more.

"I should be no more than an hour or so," I told her.

"I'll be ready by then," she said, as I was about to walk out the door to take care of my responsibilities. Although Sue was drowsy and weary as I told her my immediate plans, she alertly called out, almost angry, "No good morning kiss?"

What else could I do?

I was the first customer of the day at the VW dealership. The mechanic who worked on my car was in his early twenties, and was a student at the University of Wyoming in Laramie. It took us no time to hit it off. I told him the car was rebuilt in Salt Lake City, and now it needed a valve adjustment and an oil change. I told him the story of what happened to Sue and I since we left California. I gave him a joint which he appreciated very much, but I made him promise not to smoke it until he finished working on my car.

THERES NO VACATION FROM DESIRE

It only took him a half hour to do what he had to do, and then we took her for a short test run out near the highway. He gave me some good advice, and said, "With maintenance these Volkswagen motors can last a life time. I'm not kidding you, partner". He drove back to the garage as we smoked the joint I gave him.

He reported to his boss that my car was in A-1 shape, perfect condition, and could go from now till doomsday. You'd never know he was stoned. I had confidence in his remarks because of the expertise he displayed while working on my car.

Leaving Laramie that morning Sue and I both noticed that the terrain was changing drastically. We were coming down out of the mountains and into the foothills. Later in the day, by the time we were passing Cheyenne the land was small rolling hills, and flat in some stretches. We were definitely out of the mountain atmosphere and into the aura of the plains. The big green sign on the side of the road read WELCOME TO NEBRASKA.

Our basketball team at Great Plains University came to Nebraska to play Norfolk, and we won. From now on every state we passed through was familiar and felt like home to me. The foreign mountain region was gone. We'd passed through the desert, then over the mountains, and now nothing but a thousand miles of flat, rolling, gentle farmland, where the roads are straight and level and would put a minimum of strain on the Bug. She'd already done the tough stuff though and I had a lot of confidence in her.

Sue and I kissed hard and we felt great, and we even looked for a place where we could make love, but we finally decided to keep on chugging. We had the physical evidence of the changed land to prove we were making progress. Nebraska is a very large state. It's an all day trip to cross her.

Our original plan was to drive across the entire state and try to get to Omaha that night. Omaha rests on the Nebraska-Iowa state line. I thought that to start our trek in Iowa the next morning, a state I'd been to many times and felt at home in, would be good for my morale, which was already good. We underestimated the size of the state and by the time we were nearing the town of Grand Island, about midnight, we were so tired we could hardly stay awake. You know what happens when you drive with your eyes closed?

Coasting off the ramp of the Interstate it was easy to find a motel because Grand Island is the biggest town in central Nebraska. We didn't even have to drive into town to find a cheap room. The first place we saw had a huge golden illuminated sign advertising the great rate of fifteen dollar overnights. It was a modern and clean place with all the facilities you'd find at one of the more expensive motels. It was road homogenized though, and lacked that touch of originality, the way the motel in Laramie did.

We got in so late we didn't even take advantage of watching the color television. Probably nothing on but grain reports anyway. We took a very hot shower shedding the road grime again, and when we hit the big comfortable bed we nodded off to dreamland without even making love. We slept the contented sleep of the dead that night and woke about five. Sue was even raring to go at that hour.

THERES NO VACATION FROM DESIRE

We gassed up then had a bellyful at a roadside diner before entering the ramp onto the Interstate. Driving at this time of the morning is always a pleasure. The sun hasn't risen yet and everything is cool. Things are just getting started. Nothing is in full swing yet. Everything is budding. As cars passed us on the road, I don't push mine anymore. I could see some of the passengers stretching and stirring for the first time that day. The birth of a new day has always been one of my greatest pleasures. And now, observing this commencement from a new perspective was divine.

WELCOME TO IOWA.

The trip was becoming routine to us, and the longer we drove the more confidence we gained. The weather and land were agreeing with us, and by the time we were passing Des Moines, we were hoping we'd be able to save some of the way we felt now to use in our endeavor to make a home in New York.

WELCOME TO ILLINOIS.

WELCOME TO INDIANA.

WELCOME TO OHIO.

We entered the Buckeye State late in the afternoon. I decided to spend the night at the Toledo Holiday Inn, a place I slept at a bunch of times on my travels. I wanted to stay there for old times sake, on the dawn of a new life.

Following a rosy, restful afternoon, swimming in the indoor pool, having a few drinks at the bar, then diner by candlelight in the fine motel restaurant, we retired for the night.

"You know Sue. We'll be there tomorrow. Toledo is only a days drive from New York."

"The City?" she said, eyes agog.

"Yes. We'll be there tomorrow. What do you think about that?"

END

About the Author

Bruce Jarish was born and raised in Brooklyn, New York and is a product of its public school system, graduating from Tilden High School.

He received an Associate degree in Arts from Iowa Central Community College at Fort Dodge. While at Iowa Central he lettered in football, playing on a nationally ranked junior college team. He received his Bachelor of Science degree in history from Minnesota State University in 1971. He then completed his formal education at Central Michigan University earning a Masters Degree.

Throughout the 1970's Mr. Jarish worked as a high school teacher in New York City, Mexico City and California. He was out of the education field for approximately three decades while earning a living in an assortment of odd jobs. For twenty years his primary job was a New York City cab driver.

Since 2006 Mr. Jarish has been working as a substitute teacher in the New York City public school system. He currently lives in Howard Beach, Queens, NY.

Other books available from
Lyons & Grant Multimedia LLC

Supernature by H.V.Lyons
$14.95
978-0-9837172-0-1

Supernature is a story about genetic engineering gone awry. After a series of strange incidents in the Arizona desert along with unexplained disappearances on a California beach an unlikely team of investigators and scientists join together to unravel a mystery of global proportions. Something is causing animals around the world to mutate, evolve and breed at an accelerated rate endangering the lives of thousands. It becomes a race against time to find a solution to halt the spread of the mass mutations. If they fail it could mean the end of man kind.

Chained Gun by Donny Frank
$12.95
978-0-9837172-1-8

In this Sci-Fi-Action-Western based in post-civil war America, travel with Gallie the gun, as his search for retribution leads him to confront his past and face an enemy that threatens the future of a nation.

Visit our website at www.lgmmedia.net

All major credit cards accepted

www.ingramcontent.com/pod-product-compliance
Lightning Source LLC
Chambersburg PA
CBHW031240290426
44109CB00012B/373